Conflict is everywhere in our wor
is important. Looking at conflict
ent Kind takes us on a helpful jour
book will help you think about how
it to unity and peace.

...... and potentially work through

—**Dr. Darrell L. Bock**, Executive Director for Cultural Engagement,
Howard G. Hendricks Center for Christian Leadership and
Cultural Engagement; Senior Research Professor
of New Testament Studies Dallas Theological Seminary

Oletha Barnett has wisely discerned that God has built diversity into creation in
order to give His people the opportunity to demonstrate the humility, patience,
kindness, and forbearance of Christ as we weave our differences into a beautiful tapestry of diverse gifts and callings that build the church and bless the world.

—**Ken Sande**, Founder of Peacemaker Ministries and RW360

Oletha's fresh approach to conflict resolution will be helpful in our society of a
multitude of diversity beyond race. In *Diversity of a Different Kind*, she explores
differences common to everyone that often lead to conflict. It provides great
insight and wisdom for managing division and strife. I highly recommend it.

—**Dr. Martin E. Hawkins**, President Emeritus,
Southern Bible Institute & College

Oletha Barnett has worked extensively in the area of conflict resolution, as well
as in the legal profession. With so much discussion nowadays on diversity, she
bridges the gap theologically through insightfully recognizing that diversity is
one of God's tools to teach us how to grow in unity, and how to mature as Christians. She brings a breadth of research, knowledge, and expertise to this discussion. More than that, she brings wisdom, heart, love, and care to the table. I speak
as one who has been blessed to be the beneficiary of her expertise and her care in
this vital testing ground of conflict resolution.

—**Dr. Steve Nutter**, Pastor, Community Bible Church

Diversity of a Different Kind really helped me understand that we are created for unity. God absolutely oversees our conflict assignments of bearing the cross to bring glory to the King of Kings. Oletha inspires the reader to daily unity and an eternal calling through the ministry of reconciliation. God restores His peace in our relationships through the reconciliation work of the cross. Thanks, Oletha for your diligence and faithfulness to God.

—**P. Brian Noble**, CEO of Peacemaker Ministries

Differences seem to be tearing apart families, communities, and our nation, but Barnett shows us that God designed our differences to unite and grow us. Her new book *Diversity of a Different Kind* shows us how to use our unchangeable differences (our spiritual gifts, personality, race, generation, and gender) as well as our changeable differences (our religion, politics, experiences and socioeconomics, personal preferences, and views on social justice) to bring God glory and experience joy and peace. Barnett combines her legal expertise with decades of teaching conflict resolution classes at Oak Cliff Bible Fellowship Church in Dallas to create a fresh, distinctive approach to resolving conflict. Her book is practical, timely, and peppered with biblical support. I've known Oletha for many years, first as a student, and now as a co-laborer in Christ and friend. I trust her and highly recommend *Diversity of a Different Kind.*

—**Dr. Sue G. Edwards**, Professor of Educational Ministries and Leadership Dallas Theological Seminary, Co-author of *Leading Women Who Wound*

Oletha Barnett's book reflects her careful thinking, theological education, and extensive experience in conflict resolution. She handles Scripture wisely and relies on its truth throughout the book. The key insight that diversity is part of God's good creation takes it from the realm of social theory and places it in the bright light of God's purposes and gifts. I recommend the book for anyone who is serious about following Jesus and seeking help in navigating the challenges of conflict.

—**Karen Heetderks Strong**, PhD, Co-author of *Restoring Justice: An Introduction to Restorative Justice* and former board chair for Peacemaker Ministries

Diversity of a Different Kind may well have been entitled *Sanctification Through Ordinary Differences*. Using everyday language and very relatable stories, Barnett presents the complex nature of the Holy Spirit's work of sanctification in our lives through the diversity of God's creation. She highlights the opportunities we Christians have, to respond to diversity in a way that benefits ourselves and those around us. With a biblical roadmap to reconciliation, she challenges each Christian to live out their vocation in the ministry of reconciliation."

—**Dwight Schettler**, President, Ambassadors of Reconciliation

A veteran peacemaker and certified Christian conciliator, Oletha Barnett asserts a simple but profound point: God created us as diverse people so we might learn to become more like Christ and grow in spiritual unity and maturity. She then insightfully and boldly describes a dozen types of differences that often divide people but need not do so if we follow her biblical counsel…. She repeatedly directs us to God and His Word as the power source for gospel peace and unity amid our differences.

—**Dr. Robert D. Jones**, The Southern Baptist Theological Seminary,
author of *Uprooting Anger, Pursuing Peace*,
and co-author of *The Gospel for Disordered Lives*

Oletha Barnett has written a must-read book for anyone committed to spiritual growth and reconciliation. Read this book and learn, among many things, how God uses our differences to grow us. By the end of the book, your heart, spirit, and mind will truly view conflict and diversity differently.

—**Faith Johnson**, Retired Texas State District Judge
and Former Dallas County District Attorney

An easy read turns into an important read. As I read Barnett's latest offering of rich ministry experience and Godly wisdom, that is how I felt. It is hard to think of something more important than the health of a local church for both her leaders and congregation. *Diversity of a Different Kind* offers wise counsel toward both the individual/leader and the congregation as a Body.

In her introduction we read, *"God designed diversity to grow us into Christlikeness."* It could not be said more profoundly. For the following 178 pages, she describes through stories, illustrates and instructs from Scripture, and provides examples from her personal life (one example of which I am in), bringing this challenging subject to life.

We are all impacted by our upbringing. Our bent toward sinful actions is only surpassed by how boldly we hold to sinful attitudes. Barnett's reminder and exhortation to focus on Christlikeness goes far beyond the typical approach to diversity. Instead of seeing differences (clearly present), to see unity! My how the Church needs this message.

—Paul Cornwell,
Co-founder Crossroads Resolution Group
Certified Relational Conciliator
Certified Christian Conciliator

DIVERSITY

OF A

DIFFERENT

KIND

OLETHA J. BARNETT

To my mom and dad, Sylvester Wendell Barnett and Nina Jeffers Barnett, for their love and training. I am grateful that God chose you to be my parents. Thank you!

ACKNOWLEDGMENTS

HIGHEST ACKNOWLEDGMENT:

To God for giving me Jesus and a fresh perspective and approach to resolving conflict, culminating in this book.

It took a village to get me here.

THE VILLAGE:

- If you missed the dedication page to my parents, I again acknowledge my mom and dad, Sylvester Wendell Barnett and Nina Jeffers Barnett; double honor to you. And to my brothers and sisters for our close bond, the first people with whom I had a conflict—excellent training ground! Love you!

- Special acknowledgment to my sister Ruth Barnett, who I had told for years, there are books inside me. She would say, "Girl, write the books." I didn't. Then one day, she spurred me on by getting up in my face and saying, "Look, if you die before me, I don't want to look down at the ground and say, "books in the ground." No books in the ground! God willing, more books to come.

- To my sister Sharon Dawson for our prayer times together.

- To Dr. Martin Hawkins, who God used to start me on my conflict resolution ministry journey. It is not possible to state how much he has helped me and all that I have learned from him over the years.

- To my pastor of 30 years, Dr. Tony Evans, from whom I learn weekly and more often when I read his books. He continues to give me the great privilege of serving as the Reconciliation Director at Oak Cliff Bible Fellowship.

- To Shirley Hawkins, teacher extraordinaire, from whom I learned much about teaching and developing presentations.

- To my friend Jean Stubblefield Sims, who permitted me to use her poem in this book titled, "Let It Go."

- To Doug and Barbara Smith, who were the first to introduce me to the idea of writing a book to the best of my recollection.

- To Braque and Linda Wilson, my friends of 50 years, for encouragement to finish the book.

- To every mediator and support staff with whom I have ever had the privilege to work within the Reconciliation ministry at Oak Cliff Bible Fellowship.

- To Sylvia Stewart, who had the foresight to tell me that I needed a book Foreword as a new author. Wow! Look what I would have missed without that foresight. And thank you for your laughter over the years.

- To Terri Cooper, whose statement that "God is strategic" impacted my thinking for the book.

- To all the peacemaking family of fellow-laborers of Peacemaker Ministries, Relational Wisdom 360, Ambassadors of Reconciliation, Crossroads Resolution group, and all other groups and individuals. Keep going! May our tribe increase.

- To every Sunday school teacher, Bible teacher, pastor, and Dallas seminary professor from whom I learned.

- To my friend, John Fortner, who referred me to the great editor, Georgia Varozza, who referred me to the great graphic designer, Steve Kuhn, who referred me to my great web developer, Kathleen Istudor. Thank you for your part in the production of this book. I needed you.

FOR THEIR KEEN INSIGHT AND INTERACTION WITH THE MANUSCRIPT

- To Pastor Marcus Bellamy, Dr. Tim Fuller, and Sherbert Mims.

- To Shirley Hawkins and Shirley Walker for their interaction with my earlier manuscript, which led to *Diversity of a Different Kind.*

PRAYER WARRIORS

- Most of the people already acknowledged also pray for me, so I won't mention their names again. But, to these, my friends who not only pray for me, but all my sisters and brothers, nieces and nephews and cousins: Thank you, Alice Williams, Linda Bailey, Joan Watson, Faith Johnson, Gracie Lewis, and Sherbert Mims. I have heart-felt gratitude that after decades you still have my family members on your prayer lists.

- And to the prayer group at Oak Cliff Bible Fellowship (my first ministry there) is committed to praying for others. Continue to pray without ceasing.

JEFFERS/BARNETT CLAN

To the descendants of L.D. and Ophelia Jeffers (Mom's parents) and Frank and Francis Barnett (Dad's parents). For those saved family, pray for the unsaved family. Bring them in!

CONTENTS

FOREWORD

by Dr. Tony Evans

Oletha Barnett is one of those unsung heroes of the faith who plays a strategic role in the Kingdom of God. Her uniqueness lies in how she has kingdomized her legal background to help develop and lead the reconciliation ministry at our church in Dallas.

Scripture is clear that matters of division and differences are to be handled by the church, not secular courts. Oletha leads teams of mature believers in hearing disputes between members and seeking to bring reconciliation, healing, and unity out of conflict. And yes, when necessary, church discipline when required due to sinful rebellion.

On a regular basis Oletha adjudicates cases referred to her and her team that allows us to be the church and not just talk church. As other churches and ministries have become aware of this aspect of our ministry, Oletha is being called upon to help them understand the biblical and necessary process for churches to apply God's principles of reconciliation in their ministries.

God uses our diversity, differences, and even our disputes to grow us spiritually into mature followers of Christ. This book is essential reading for believers and Christian leaders who desire to utilize God's method of addressing our various diversities in a righteous manner without denying the uniqueness that has been given to us by our Creator.

Diversity of a Different Kind is one of those one-of-a-kind books that will open up to the reader a new paradigm for healing wounds, restoring relationships, addressing and correcting sin, and unifying the church that is so desperately needed today. In a world rife with the issues of division of every kind, this special work will show how God's people operating on God's principles can bring God's solution to a broken culture starting with the church.

Dr. Tony Evans
President, The Urban Alternative
Senior Pastor, Oak Cliff Bible Fellowship

DIVERSITY OF A DIFFERENT KIND

D*iversity of a Different Kind* gives a unique viewpoint to resolve conflict. When we hear the word diversity, we may think of racial issues; however, God created diversity far beyond race. In this book, I explore over a dozen differences common to man and explain how God not only can use diversity to grow us but designed it for that purpose. *Diversity of a Different Kind* consists of two aspects: (1) different perspective, and (2) different approach to conflict resolution.

The different perspective is that God designed diversity to grow us into Christlikeness. The different approach is to embrace God's divine design of diversity for its benefit. Within His created differences, He set in motion the potential for naturally arising circumstances to give us opportunities to practice biblical principles for moral advance. He set us up to grow us up. Growth in turn gives us the wisdom we need to unify instead of divide. Throughout the book, we give details and evidence of how diversity is designed to grow us and thereby produce the byproduct of unifying us. Enjoy the unique journey.

PART 1

DIVERSITY PERSPECTIVE

Humanity is diverse, dynamic, and complex.

CHAPTER 1

ALLOW FOR THE DIFFERENCES OF OTHERS

Things are not always what they seem.

FROM POEM, "MUCH TO LEARN"

The majority of people do not think the way you think. What is wrong with them? Nothing. Nor is anything wrong with you. I learned the truth of the fact that the majority do not think like I (or you) do when I attended Dallas Theological Seminary.

PERSPECTIVES LESSON

In a Christian education class, two professors gave us a learning styles test. Learning styles indicate how our minds take in and process information, how we communicate, and how we teach. Based on our test results, the professors grouped us into four categories with those who tested like-minded. Then, they gave each group the same class assignment: Jointly prepare to tell the rest of the class how to best teach your group. My group quickly completed the task and talked about other things as we waited for the others to finish. After a period, we noticed the other groups continued to work well beyond the time we spent. My group quietly chuckled at how slowly the others worked.

The longer they worked, the more we laughed. The last group took such a long time to finish that we made comments out of their hearing. "What could they be doing that would take that long?" I saw the two professors smile at each other as they watched us. They knew what behavior to expect from each group and in what order each group would finish the task.

Was my group smarter than the other group? No. We merely processed differently. My group tested as "Analytic" learners. Analytic learners are bottom-line people, which accounts for why we finished first. The group that finished last and appeared to struggle most tested as "Collaborative" learners.

Collaborative learners work to get everyone on the same page. They learn best when they collaborate with others. I was surprised to hear Collaborative learners not only need to collaborate, but they enjoy the process. My group misunderstood how their group processes and communicates. We thought they struggled with the assignment, whereas they liked the process.

Scores of learning style studies exist. The learning styles test we took was from Bernice McCarthy's instructional method that identified four categories. The third category consists of "Dynamic" learners, who are visionaries. They see things in their minds, dream, and love to experiment. The fourth group, "Common Sense" learners, like to pursue practical solutions.

I do not intend to teach learning styles but to illustrate how people think and communicate differently. Through the assignment, the professors sought to educate us to understand students' differences, so we could develop lesson plans to allow each type of learner to maximize learning.

Collaborative learners would feel frustration and struggle if a bottom-line teacher only taught the bottom line. People generally teach based on their own learning style, in disregard of the various styles of learners. I assessed the classroom activity and saw how misunderstandings could cause conflict. What if the collaborative learners had heard us laugh at them and became offended? Our behavior could have led to a conflict based on a lack of understanding of our differences.

LENSES THROUGH WHICH WE LOOK

The lenses through which we look color what we see. I am nearsighted. If I put on farsighted lenses, my vision would become skewed. We all have perspectives regarding life, people, and diversity. My learning style group looked through myopic lenses. We did not have telescopic lenses to see far enough to allow for differences. We need the different assemblies that God designed, just the way He made each. We are better together with differences, skills, and insights. We need the creativeness of the Dynamic learner to envision it. We need Common Sense learners to show us how to best make practical use of it. We need Collaborative learners to try to keep the peace as we work together. We need the Analytic learners to help move the project along and then say, what's next. If an army general is in a heated battle, we need quick, bottom-line decisions as the enemy approaches. The battle would be a loss if the general stopped to collaborate. On the other hand, if a situation requires collaboration, we do not need bottom-line thinkers.

DIFFERING PERSPECTIVES
CAN LEAD TO CONFLICT

Let's revisit my original statement. The majority of people do not think the way you think. Based on the test results, we ended up in 4 groups, wherein about 25% of the class was in each group. Our outcome reflected the norm for the test results: approximately 25% of people fall into each category. Thus, in whatever group you land, 75% of people will test in the three other groups. Hence, the majority of the people do not think as you think. Neither process is right or wrong, merely different. Our differences often lead to conflict. I define conflict in terms of relationships. Conflict is differences that result in disharmony in relationships.

How aware are you that you either just left a conflict, you are in conflict, or you are headed to a conflict? The boxer Joe Louis said, "You can run, but you can't hide." Or as the "Bad Boys" song says, "Bad boys, bad boys, what you gonna do when they come for you?"[1] Conflict is coming for you. According to N.E. Algert, on average, people engage in 5 conflicts daily. It is possible to have a conflict at home, work, and in your leadership position at the same time. In fact, you can have multiple conflicts in each area at the same time. You will want to count the cost of your engagement in conflict. At first glance, 5 conflicts daily may seem large, but when you look at our culture, some people appear to engage in conflict continuously. The way we engage in conflict to some degree is learned behavior. I went with a friend to visit her mother in another city. I observed the same combative behavior in the mother that I saw in the friend, including the negative facial expressions and tone of voice. We are sometimes unsuccessful in conflict engagement because we do not know how to handle conflict. We will help you learn to manage conflict in diverse situations throughout the book.

THE NATURE OF CONFLICT

The nature of a thing is the character of a thing. Birds fly. Frogs hop. Fish swim. It is within their nature to do so. There are three things about the nature of conflict. You already heard the first one above. Conflict is unavoidable. Second: Conflict can kill peace. Third: Conflict can be a channel to increase peace. Though somewhat different, I use the terms oneness, unity, peace, and harmony interchangeably throughout the book.

Conflict can happen suddenly, and we get caught off guard. Diversity is one of our primary sources of conflict. God's diversity abounds well beyond race, which we will see as we explore differences. We interact with a myriad of differences within complex human dynamics. This book presupposes your desire to live in a way that honors God in every area of your life. For that goal, recognize the supremacy of God's Word for all aspects of life, including of course, conflict resolution—the focus of this book.

THE NEED TO CURTAIL CONFLICT

Scripture is replete with passages to seek peace and live in peace (See Romans 14:19, Ephesians 4:3, 1 Peter 3:11, Psalm 34:14, 2 Corinthians

13:11). So, one reason you want to curtail conflict is in obedience to God to seek peace and live in unity and harmony. It makes for better societal living and brings blessings to the peacemaker (see Matthew 5:9).

ALLOW FOR DIFFERENCES

After the class activity, I thought about a former employee who some wished could get to the point and not go on. He was a Collaborative processor, though I was not familiar with the terminology at that time. My learning journey brought me to a conflict resolution principle: "Allow for the Differences of Others." When we allow for differences, we will more likely treat one another with the respect and dignity that everyone deserves. It also helps reduce conflict. I want to be unequivocally clear; I am not talking about embracing sinful differences. I speak of respecting (1) people and (2) different opinions that are not sinful. Of course, you also allow for sin that exists, but don't embrace the sin. Love the person; hate the bad conduct because it violates God's standards.

God wants His people unified, not in conflict. Though I cover many characteristics in *Diversity of a Different Kind*, I focus primarily on three areas. The first is spiritual growth. I use interchangeably the terms spiritual growth, spiritual maturity, holiness, and grow to be like Christ. These terms refer to advancement in moral character because we can never be like Christ in His transcendent holiness. Second, I focus on unity, oneness, and peace, which I also use interchangeably. They are byproducts of Christlike growth. Third, I focus on love, the nature and character of God, which we need for righteous living. All three—Spiritual growth, unity, and love—all fall under the umbrella of glorifying God.

The reason glorifying God is so important is because it is the very reason God created us. "Everyone who is called by my name, whom I created for my glory, whom I formed and made" (Isaiah 43:7; see also 1 Corinthians 10:31). When we pursue unity and harmony in our interactions with others, we fulfill one of God's purposes for us. We cannot fulfill God's purposes for our lives if we do not grow spiritually. The mature Christian will use wisdom for unity and peace. Through growth, we learn to love and live in unity.

Disallowance of differences leads to social disruption. In Colossians 3, the apostle Paul provides a clear perspective of how we should live socially, regardless of our created differences. He focuses on holy and pure living for individuals and the church. Paul analogizes wrongful and rightful behavior to changing clothes. He instructs to take off the clothes of anger, rage, malice, slander, filthy language, and lying and to put on clothes of compassion, kindness, humility, gentleness, and patience.

We see the principle of allowing for the differences of others in Colossians 3, "Bear with each other and forgive one another if any of you has a grievance against someone. Forgive as the Lord forgave you. And over all these virtues put on love, which binds them all together in perfect unity" (Colossians 3:13-14). When we let love cover our social interactions, we honor God. We cannot understand the meaning of life without God's Word. Colossians 3:15-16 instructs us to have hearts full of God's Word, peace, and good will toward one another. Christ called us into unity and peace. We can do that through putting aside differences to bear with one another. The way we see the world and life is our worldview. When a believer sees through a biblical worldview, our perspective aligns with God's standards, the grid that gives clear vision.

Much to Learn

Things are not always what they seem;
When we open our eyes, we see life; not a dream.

The world is expansive, not myopic;
We can learn about many topics.

Embrace the possibilities.
Relinquish insensibilities.
Allow for the differences.

CHAPTER 2

DIVERSITY THEORY

*Call to me and I will answer you and tell you great
and unsearchable things you do not know.*

JEREMIAH 33:3

We are precious in God's sight. He made us in His image and breathed life into us. He redeemed us and focuses His love on us. He plans to prosper us not harm us (see Jeremiah 29:11). So great is His loving care for us to advance spiritually that He superintends our growth. Moreover, He set up a diverse universal system for us to grow, which I refer to as "diversity theory." *Diversity theory is the belief that God created human diversity to give us naturally arising opportunities to practice biblical principles to produce Christlike character growth.*

God wants oneness for His church. The naturally arising encounters can result in conflict if we operate from our sinful nature. On the other hand, when we operate righteously, the encounter results in peace and harmony. From the many examples provided in this book, you will see diversity as a source for growth and unity.

Growth brings righteous living, which impedes the devil from disrupting our lives. No matter the diverse encounter, we can submit to God and be led by God's Spirit within to help us make the right decisions. During conflict, some of the principles we can practice include humility, gentleness, patience, love, confession, and forgiveness to glorify God and keep us unified. Whatever the case, God mandates that we pursue peace. "So, then we pursue the things which make for peace and the building up of one another" (Romans 14:19).

We have heard God loves diversity; all we have to do is look around to behold the beauty of His created diversity. Yes, God loves diversity, but He is also strategic. He can love diversity and have an additional divine purpose for it. I have a beautiful burgundy leather sofa in my living room that I like. It is not there just because I like the way it looks, but it also serves a functional purpose. I believe God created diversity for more than merely because He loves variety. He is deliberate and strategic. I believe He designed human differences more to make us holy than just because He loves diversity.

God's chief aim is for us to be holy; conform to Christ. He gave us all we need to bring us to His plan of spiritual growth. He gave us Jesus, Scripture, the Holy Spirit and more to help us live successfully. He also gave us human diversity. Diverse encounters provide opportunities to practice biblical principles and thereby grow us. Through growth, we learn to confess, forgive, love, and unify. He designed us for oneness.

ORIGIN OF DIVERSITY THEORY

I read a book by Gary Thomas titled *Sacred Marriage*. Thomas posed the question, "What if God made marriage to make us holy more than to make us happy?" I woke one morning with the thought: God designed diversity to make us holy. I don't recall thinking about Thomas's book before I went to bed, but I woke with an analogous idea related to a different topic. It must have germinated in my subconscious.

I struggled with the concept for months; "What if God designed human diversity to make us holy more than just because He loves diversity?" Eventually, I went to a theologian I trust. I gave my theory and asked if he had ever heard it before. He said no. I then asked if it is theologically sound. He said yes. Although he said it is theologically sound, I was still nervous because I had not heard of it before and he had not heard of it.

Finally, I decided to go to my pastor, Dr. Tony Evans. The Bible says establish matters with two or three witnesses (see Deuteronomy

9:15, Matthew 18:16, 2 Corinthians 13:1). I was somewhat apprehensive. Dr. Evans had been my pastor for over 30 years; I did not want him to think I had grabbed ahold of heretical thinking. I gave him the theory and asked the same questions. Have you heard this before? He said no. I then asked him if it was theologically sound. He said yes. I felt relief, I had my three witnesses. Dr. Evans also said, "You are grappling with it at a high level." I knew I struggled, but the words "grappling with it at a high level" made me realize I needed clarity from God to bring it to more explicit focus. If it were not completely clear to me, I would not be able to make it clear to others. *Diversity of a Different Kind* is the culmination of God unraveling it for me, not all at once or in chunks, but bit by bit, like spoon feeding an infant.

SET UP TO GROW UP

Based on societal norms, when we hear the word "diversity," we often think of racial issues, but not here. This book gives a distinctive perspective and approach to resolving conflict. Differences tend to be the source of much conflict—personality, gender, race, age group, religion, etc. In *The Path of a Peacemaker*, P. Brian Noble, Chief Executive Officer of Peacemaker Ministries, makes the statement "The world is one tense place." Indeed it is, much of it due to diversity. Do you suppose God foreknew that His created diversity would be the source of much conflict? Of course, He did. Well, since He wants us to live in peace, what in the world could He have been thinking? God tactically created diversity not just because He loves it but to make us holy and unify us. Diversity encounters can help us grow. He set us up to grow us up. When we are spiritually mature, we live a fuller life. We apply biblical principles and can fulfill God's divine plan for our lives, which includes loving one another and living in peace and unity.

DESIGNED FOR ONENESS

All believers are one body in Christ. God wants us united, not divided. Scripture further admonishes us to "Make every effort to keep the unity of the Spirit through the bond of peace" (Ephesians 4:3). We cannot "keep" what we do not have. "Keep the unity" means to maintain what we have. Our unity lies in the fact that we have accepted Christ as Lord, which makes us God's family, one family. Whereas God desires unity; the devil desires disunity. Christ comes to give us more abundant life; the devil comes to steal, kill, and destroy us (see John 10:10).

SPIRITUAL GROWTH THROUGH ADVERSITY

God accomplishes our moral progress through various ways. The one I focus on is trials and adversity, which build character. The following story helps illustrate how adversity gives us perseverance for life issues.

Several people traveled across a large field of varying terrain. Each carried a heavy, wide cross that extended from their shoulders to the ground. Each had the personal duty to travel under the weight of their cross. As they proceeded across the field, one of them continuously complained during the journey. He bent down crying, "Lord, it's too heavy. Please cut it down." God cut his cross down, and he continued his travel, happy for the reduced weight but lagging behind the others from the cut-down stop. He continued the cycle of begging God to cut it a little more until he carried a small cross with barely any weight.

Our traveler with the short cross saw ahead a vast chasm in the ground. The gulf was so huge that you risked the danger of falling into a deep canyon if you tried to walk across or run and jump across. The other travelers used their long, wide crosses as a bridge by laying them across the divide to walk over to the other side of the gulf. Not so for the complainer; his cross was too short.

Cross bearing works for our good because it gives us fortitude for the gulf issues of life, wherein we build character and develop perseverance and hope. Indeed we should have joy in suffering knowing it will grow us. "Not only so, but we also glory in our sufferings, because we know that suffering produces perseverance; perseverance, character; and character, hope" (Romans 5:3-4). Romans 8 tells us in other language that trials are good for us. "And we know that in all things God works for the good of those who love him, who have been called according to his purpose" (Romans 8:28). When you read Romans 8:29 along with Romans 8:28, you see that the "good" is the transformation into Christlikeness. Notice also from Romans 8:28, the prerequisite for God to work the circumstances for our good is that we love Him. We show love not just with words, but by our actions (See 1 John 3:18). God works in our life circumstances for beneficial outcome. His plan is to change us from our natural inclination to what He wants for us, holiness. Though none of us like hardships, it is a part of our moral growth.

Since He sent Christ to die for us, why wouldn't He help us with our spiritual growth? He will. Nothing can separate us from His love (see Romans 8:38-39). We must grow through trials. Even Jesus learned obedience from suffering on earth. "Son though he was, he learned obedience from what he suffered" (Hebrews 5:8). Expect to suffer but also expect deliverance. God delivers us from every trial (see Psalm 34:19). He gave us the Holy Spirit to generate spiritual virtues in us for us to be more like Christ (see Romans 15:13, Galatians 5:22-23, 1 Thessalonians 1:6). The continual process of God working in us to deliver us from sin's power to Christlikeness is called sanctification. The sanctifying work of the Holy Spirit in us is ongoing and gradual.

SPIRITUAL GROWTH THROUGH DISCIPLINE

Sometimes we have hardships because God disciplines us because of sin. A loving father corrects bad behavior of his children (see Hebrews 12:5-11). Discipline is good for us as it works to transform us into Christlikeness. It produces righteousness that leads to peace and unity. "My son do not make light of the Lord's discipline, and do not lose heart when he rebukes you, because the Lord disciplines the one he loves, and he chastens everyone he accepts as his son (Hebrews 12:5-6). Whether due to natural trials or discipline, both work together for our good in producing spiritual growth. Diversity theory is linked to our spiritual growth.

DIVERSITY RUB

Let's hypothetically look at a naturally arising encounter that has the potential for conflict due to differences. It could be a personality difference, learning styles difference, or other difference. What should you do? Look at the decision regarding how to handle a diversity encounter as being at a crossroad. Which road do you take? There are two choices. One leads to friction; the other leads to the pursuit of peace. However you phrase it, we choose between good or evil, right or wrong, and godliness or ungodliness. Though two forces exist, they are not equal and opposite. The devil is a defeated foe. God is greater and God's Spirit is in us (see 1 John 4:4). The devil only has power because we give him power. The improper handling of a diversity encounter is called diversity rub. *Diversity rub* is sinful intolerance of others and their differences.

Diversity rub produces friction. It is like rubbing two sticks together that causes heat that smolders and then becomes fire. Rubbing differences against our sin nature makes a conflict fire. Such conflict fires are tied to intolerance of others' differences. When we rub differences against our godly nature, peace results. Rubbing sticks together can be likened to rubbing shoulders with others as we go through life. Conflict fires erupt when we handle interactions inappropriately.

The parties to a diversity encounter can respond differently or the same. One person can rub the difference against his sin nature and produce a conflict fire. The other can do the same, which brings us two roaring fires. Not good. Another scenario is that one person can rub against sin nature; the other person can tolerate the differences to pursue peace. Even though one person chooses to fight, it produces a better result than two fires. It is difficult to fight alone. "Without wood a fire goes out; without a gossip a quarrel dies down. As charcoal to embers and as wood to fire, so is a quarrelsome person for kindling strife" (Proverbs 26:20-21). We are not responsible for the actions of others for peacemaking, only our own actions. Scripture tells us we have a personal responsibility to try to make peace with everyone. "If it is possible, as far as it depends on you, live at peace with everyone" (Romans 12:18).

In diversity encounters, if both people tolerate each other and allow for their differences, we get the desired outcome of peace despite differences. We do not speak of tolerance of sin but of bearing with the person and allowing for differing perspectives. Nonetheless, whether the person sins or has a different non-sinful opinion, we should handle both encounters in a God-honoring way. Respect others and allow for differences. The encounter can help build our character and grow us.

DIVERSITY EMBRACE

God's ways are high above our ways (see Isaiah 55:9). He is the creator; we are the created. He is perfect, infinite, all knowing, all powerful, and present everywhere, yet He tolerates us. We are made in His image and likeness, yet we don't tolerate one another. We should embrace one another and tolerate one another as God tolerates us. *Diversity embrace* is defined as godly tolerance of others and their differences.

Through diversity embrace, we accept the other person as one who is also made in God's image and tolerate different perspectives to maintain and promote unity. There is a difference between loving a person and detesting their actions, like the good parent we mentioned who corrects bad behavior. God requires us to bear with one another, and allow for others' differences, addressed in Ephesians 4 and Colossians 3. Both speak of bearing with one another, loving and forgiving.

> As a prisoner for the Lord, then, I urge you to live a life worthy of the calling you have received. Be completely humble and gentle; be patient, bearing with one another in love. Make every effort to keep the unity of the Spirit through the bond of peace (Ephesians 4:1-3).

> Bear with each other and forgive one another if any of you has a grievance against someone. Forgive as the Lord forgave you. And over all these virtues put on love, which binds them all together in perfect unity (Colossians 3:13-14).

If you never had a conflict, you would not know how to resolve a conflict for yourself or help others resolve conflict. If we profess

Christianity, we should practice it, not merely say it (see James 1:22). When we follow Ephesians 4:2 to be completely humble, it strips us of pride, the root of sin. Ephesians 4:2 tells us that the love key is required to open the door for us to bear with one another. Ephesians 4:3 tells us we maintain peace through the bond of love. The love bond is like glue bonding to hold together love and peace. Thus, love and peace are inseparably connected.

God orchestrates events behind the scenes for His desired outcome. Look at the book of Ruth as an example. We see His hands behind the scenes orchestrating events. He brought Naomi and her diverse daughter-in-law, Ruth (a Moabite), out of famine and preserved the lineage of a king who would be the greatest king in Israel, David, and ultimately the earthly lineage of the greatest King ever, Jesus. We also see God behind the scenes in the book of Esther where He orchestrates the salvation of the Jews from threatened destruction. He continues to orchestrate events in our lives today. Within His created diversity, God set in motion the potential for naturally arising or self-generating circumstances to give us the opportunity to practice biblical principles to mature spiritually. When we grow from the encounter, we learn to keep peace, a byproduct of spiritual growth. We can take the tolerant road by bearing with others and allowing for differing perspectives without battle.

Cooperate with God during diversity encounters. He knows our hearts and whether we are obedient to Him, outwardly and inwardly. He actively looks to our activities so He can bless us. "For the eyes of the LORD range throughout the earth to strengthen those whose hearts are fully committed to him" (2 Chronicles 16:9).

PART 2

MANAGING DIFFERENCES

The three-pronged approach to managing differences is covered in this section.

1. Accept a diversity encounter as an assignment from God.

2. Serve as a minister of reconciliation to bring peace.

3. Follow biblical principles to properly interrelate with others.

CHAPTER 3

DIVERSITY ASSIGNMENTS

I n school, teachers give assignments. They give the assignments based on what they want us to learn. Assignments benefit us by helping us learn and grow. We have a duty to complete the tasks within the assignments.

GOD GIVES US ASSIGNMENTS

God's love and desire for us to grow far exceeds that of any other teacher. He also gives us assignments, some of which are diversity encounters. *A diversity encounter is a divine assignment from God, which gives us opportunities to practice biblical principles for growth.* I remind you of the other diversity definitions again for ease of use in this chapter.

- *Diversity theory* is the belief that God created human diversity to give us naturally arising opportunities to practice biblical principles to produce Christlike character growth.

- *Diversity rub* is sinful intolerance of others and their differences.

- *Diversity embrace* is defined as godly tolerance of others and their differences.

Underneath the diversity assignment umbrella is an opportunity for us to work toward unity and harmony for God's glory. We have a duty to complete assignments from God, which He gives to refine us and teach us lessons of love, unity, and other lessons. When we do not work with others through diverse encounters, we lose by failing to complete an assignment designed to grow us. During growth assignments, we learn to improve interactions with people of different temperaments and enhance our conflict management skills. We can also learn to take responsibility for contributions we might make to the conflict.

After we complete assignments, God tests us on what we learned. The better we complete the day-to-day assignments, the better we do on tests. It is for our good and God's glory. You may say to a regular teacher, "I messed up. May I retake the test?" Although you may ask for a make-up test from your teacher, the teacher may not give one. It is unnecessary to request a make-up test from the Perfect Teacher. He is so interested in our growth that He gives it to us without our inquiry. If we become disappointed in how we handled an assignment or test from God, regret is useful. It can spur the desire to do better the next time.

When God tests our faith, it produces perseverance in us; fortitude for life (see James 1:3). It prepares us for greater service and is necessary for our spiritual well-being. When we withstand our perseverance assignments, we receive a reward in judgment: "Blessed is the one who perseveres under trial because, having stood the test, that person will receive the crown of life that the Lord has promised to those who love him" (James 1:12). Because of our growth and God's promises to reward perseverance, we can face trials with joy. "Consider it pure joy, my brothers and sisters, whenever you face trials of many kinds, because you know that the testing of your faith produces perseverance" (James 1:2-3). The reason we can count it joy is because of the assurance we will pass the tests, though we may have to retake tests several times before passage. God sits as the refiner to help us through the purification process. We prove what is good and acceptable to Christ (Romans 12:1).

Scripture further teaches us that the trials that God carries us through are beneficial, like a parent disciplining a child for the child's well-being (see Hebrews 12). As Peter reminds us, "Dear friends, do not be surprised at the fiery ordeal that has come on you to test you, as though something strange were happening to you" (1 Peter 4:12). The purpose is to purify; to separate the gold from the dross. This can only happen when metal is heated to an extremely high temperature.

Sometimes, I feel like saying, "God, can You just develop me another way?" But God reminds me it is His way, not mine; His will, not mine. He knows what we need better than we know. Some adversity is the order of the day for our spiritual growth. After we successfully complete assignments and tests, we move to the next level, including helping others with what we learned.

GOD SUPERINTENDS ASSIGNMENTS HE GIVES

I became excited when I learned that God superintends our growth through life's trials like a refiner for silver and gold (see Proverbs 17:3, Isaiah 48:10, Malachi 3:3, Job 23:10). He did not send a second lieutenant or a 5-star general. The one who made the lieutenant, the general, and everyone else, oversees our growth. A refiner puts raw silver or gold in a scorching furnace until the impurities float to the top. The refiner skims off the trash and repeats the fiery furnace process until he can see his reflection in the silver or gold, which signifies the purity. That is what God looks for in us. He desires to see Christ's image reflected when He looks at our lives, to signify the fiery trial we went through purified us. That is why we have burdens to bear, crosses to carry, and adversity in life, including the fire of conflict.

Conflict is not our problem. The problem is the condition of our hearts that needs purification to lead us to appropriately manage conflict encounters. Diversity assignments benefit us by being means to growth. Growth can turn hard hearts to warm, caring hearts. Even when we fail, God continues to patiently superintend our growth. Remember our illustration in a previous chapter regarding the cross-bearer. When the complaining cross-bearer cried at the gulf because his cross was too short to cross over the wide gulf, Jesus laid across the gulf with arms stretched wide in cross-like fashion for the complainer to cross over. God often carries us and then places us on the ground so we will learn to walk. Babies learning to walk fall, but they keep trying and eventually walk straight and skillfully. Like the babies who don't quit, we can keep trying until we too, can walk skillfully and righteously during our diversity encounters and other life events.

Regardless of life status, adversity happens to us all. None can escape cross-bearing. Consider your current growth status and look back at the hardships and trials you experienced. As you evaluate your hardships history, you will realize you grew through adversity and gained more fortitude and stamina for life issues. This realization should help us embrace diversity assignments. That is the approach for diversity encounters. Embrace it. Bear with others and their differences (See Colossians 3:13).

When going through a trial, we can get to the point of recognizing the assignment will work for our good during the assignment, not just realizing it after the fact. That is when you know to embrace the assignment and count it joy because of the benefit, which is our recurring theme of the encounter working together for our good (see Romans 8:28). When we successfully complete assignments related to our differences, we receive many byproducts: fortitude for life, peace, spiritual growth, improved relationship with God and fellow man.

SPIRITUAL GROWTH EXAMPLE

A woman was invited to speak at a conference for 4 consecutive years. Each year she prayed for the conference. Below is a brief scenario of her prayer. The prayers show how she progressively grew from year to year.

- Year 1: God bless my presentation at the conference. Let me outshine everyone else.

- Year 2: God bless me and all the other speakers at the conference.

- Year 3: God bless me and all the speakers at the conference and all aspects of the conference

- Year 4: God bless all the speakers, hearers, and everything associated with the conference for Your glory.

UNCOMFORTABLE CONFLICT ASSIGNMENTS

Godliness is profitable. "For physical training is of some value, but godliness has value for all things, holding promise for both the present life and the life to come" (1 Timothy 4:8). Yet, we are not on a Sunday School picnic. We are God's laborers, which can bring us uncomfortable assignments. The story about Titus and the Cretans is an example. The Cretans had false teachers who for dishonest gain endangered the church and families. They claimed to know God but acted otherwise (see Titus 1:10-16). The apostle Paul left Titus on the Greek Island of Crete to rebuke the Cretans and get them in order so they would be sound in the faith. "The reason I left you in Crete was that you might put in order what was left unfinished and appoint elders in every town, as I directed you" (Titus 1:5). You may be left in an unpleasant or uncomfortable job position, ministry situation, organizational association, or other association. Don't complain or move too quickly. You may be there for a reason, a divine assignment.

TWO WAYS TO HANDLE
DIVERSITY ASSIGNMENTS

In a previous chapter, we set out the three things about the nature of conflict. It is unavoidable; it can kill peace; it can be a channel to increase peace. Conflict is not bad in itself. It has the potential for good or bad, depending on how we handle it. We can handle conflict assignments constructively or destructively.

DESTRUCTIVE CONFLICT MANAGEMENT

Destructive conflict management aligns with diversity rub, sinful intolerance of others and their differences. When we handle conflict destructively, we give it enormous power to disrupt our lives. You have experienced it in every sphere of life and have seen its destructive impact on yourself and others. When we fail to harness conflict appropriately, we weaken relationships, can become bitter, and foster greater conflict. When we engage destructively, we sin and thereby fail to grow spiritually.

CONSTRUCTIVE CONFLICT MANAGEMENT

Constructive management of conflict aligns with diversity embrace, godly tolerance of others and their differences. It offers an opportunity for creativity, collaboration, and improvement. It strengthens relationships, improves your ability to manage conflict, and helps you grow spiritually. Constructive conflict management can positively impact individuals, families, ministries, businesses, and all levels of government and nations.

If we fail to successfully complete the assignment or test, God will test you again because He wants us to learn. When you pass the test, you can have a testimony to help others as they go through trials. If you never had a problem, you would not know the power God gives you to solve problems in a biblically faithful manner. Embrace diversity encounters. Bear with people who differ from you, grow from there, and live in peace and unity.

Within our diversity assignments, the other person may not be the wrongdoer. Assess whether a sin issue exists with you. Scripture tells us that we strain to see fault in others when we can't see clearly because we disregard the sin in our own lives. "You hypocrite, first take the plank out of your own eye, and then you will see clearly to remove the speck from your brother's eye" (Matthew 7:5).

When we ask the Holy Spirit to help us see how we might have contributed to the conflict, He will bring clarity for correction and proper engagement with others. Confess and forgive as appropriate. Be humble. When we don't get it right, God has us covered through a biblical provision: "If we confess our sins, he is faithful and just and will forgive us our sins and purify us from all unrighteousness" (1 John 1:9). A proper response brings growth; an improper response hinders growth.

End the encounter in peaceful reconciliation and unity or peacefully agree to differ on the matter. The more spiritually mature we are, the better we handle diverse conflict encounters. Below is a spiritual growth testimonial via poetry.

Fit

Use me however you see fit, has been my request.
Didn't know my cry required prep, through various tests.

The trek has been long with canyons, and ravines difficult.
Needed to build muscle, for work strength to get right result.

It has become easier, as I learned you to consult.
Following wise guidance brings result in you to exalt.

You knew which fires I would need, to make me a useful fit.
You know me for I'm your design, whom from the womb, you knit.

Now, refined through the fire for use, as you see fit.
Now, strong for service to stand brave, not run and quit.

No weak vessel soldiers needed for this trek.
They go under at every enemy peck.

In a sprint race, they offer a prize to the winner.
You groomed me to bring you glory, not me the sprinter.

You did it your way for me to be fit.
I pray I remember, and not forget.

CHAPTER 4

YOUR MINISTRY OF RECONCILIATION

At one time, I wondered about my ministry. It looked like everyone had a ministry, but I had no idea about mine. Since then, I learned that our ministry aligns with our spiritual gifts, which the Holy Spirit gives to each at the point of salvation. Though I now know my ministry, God also commissions every believer for general services, one of which is the ministry of reconciliation. "All this is from God, who reconciled us to himself through Christ and gave us the ministry of reconciliation" (2 Corinthians 5:18).

In addition to embracing the diversity encounter as an assignment from God, it is part of your ministry of reconciliation. The ministry of reconciliation is one of the approaches God desires for us to use during diversity encounters for peace and reconciliation.

RECONCILED TO GOD

To reconcile means to restore to a peaceful relationship after a period of disharmony. In short, to reconcile means to make peace. We need reconciliation because of original sin in the Garden of Eden. The Hebrew roots *ht'* expresses that sin is missing the mark, missing God's standard for righteousness. It also means to be *rāša'*, i.e., wicked or to act wickedly (see 2 Samuel 22:22; Nehemiah 9:33). The primary characteristic of sin is that it is against God; it contradicts Him and separates us from Him (see Isaiah 59:1-2). It always involves pride, which was the devil's sin (see Isaiah 14:12-14).

Before sin in the Garden of Eden, humanity was in perfect communion with God. Sin in the Garden broke man's fellowship with God, where we gave ourselves over to Satan. We had no power to correct our sinful state, so God sent Christ to die for our sins. He took the death penalty for our sin and restored our relationship with God. "God made him who had no sin to be sin for us, so that in him we might become the righteousness of God" (2 Corinthians 5:21). Thus, Christ took us from our sinful and broken fellowship with God to the right relationship with God. That is the greatest reconciliation gift of all. God reconciled us to Himself.

God did not sin and cannot sin, so He did not need to reconcile Himself to us, but needed to reconcile us to Him. It is humanity who transgressed. God is always the subject of the active verb "to reconcile" *(katallassein)*. Humans are the subject of the passive noun reconciliation *(katallagē)*. God actively reconciles. Humans are reconciled. Man did nothing and could do nothing to deserve God reconciling man to Himself, but He did it through His love for us (see John 3:16). Scripture is clear regarding God's love for us. "But God demonstrates his own love for us in this: While we were still sinners, Christ died for us" (Romans 5:8).

Through salvation, we become the family of God and are in right relationship with Him because of Jesus. The unbeliever is at enmity with God; we are not. However, when believers fail to confess and repent for our sin, we break fellowship with God. We reconcile and restore our fellowship with God by confessing and turning away from sin (see 1 John 1:9).

WHAT IS THE MINISTRY OF RECONCILIATION?

A ministry of reconciliation is how you serve to restore relationships. Ministers of reconciliation are not only preachers and pastors, but God gave all believers a ministry of reconciliation.

Therefore, if anyone is in Christ, the new creation has come: The old has gone, the new is here! All this is from God, who reconciled us to himself through Christ and gave us the ministry of reconciliation: that God was reconciling the world to himself in Christ, not counting people's sins against them. And he has committed to us the message of reconciliation. We are therefore Christ's ambassadors, as though God were making his appeal through us. We implore you on Christ's behalf: Be reconciled to God (2 Corinthians 5:17-20).

Christ commissioned us for a ministry of reconciliation, which means He gives us authority. Thus, He left us a legacy. As ministers of reconciliation, we fulfill God's plan to unify people. Ronald Reagan said, "Peace is not absence of conflict, it is the ability to handle conflict by peaceful means." We have a responsibility to carry out our ministry of reconciliation. It puts us in an ongoing position to seek peace. When we embrace diverse assignments, we can bring unity within diversity. Your ministry of reconciliation is the centerpiece for unity.

Christ's commission of us to a ministry of reconciliation is also in keeping with the great commission (see Matthew 28:18-20). He commissioned us to make disciples, bringing others to Him. He will give us various opportunities to bring others to Him as a regular part of life. Even while jailed in Philippi, Paul and Silas allowed God to use them for the conversion of the Philippian jailer and all his household (See Acts 16).

We show the gospel in our lives when we properly manage conflict. It is not only a testimony to nonbelievers but also to fellow believers when we show our Christian faith by our conduct.

There are four aspects of reconciliation. The first two relate to salvation (reconciliation to God). The last two relate to resolving conflict (reconciliation to others).

1. We accept Christ as Lord and Savior, which means we become reconciled to God (salvation).

2. We help the unregenerate become reconciled to God (salvation through evangelism).

3. We reconcile our personal conflicts with others.

4. We help people reconcile their conflict with others.

The four facets are described below in more detail.

SALVATION RECONCILIATION

1. Personal Salvation

There is no reconciliation without first being reconciled to Christ (salvation) who took the penalty for our sin. Scripture is clear that unbelievers are enemies of God (see Romans 5:10; Colossians 1:21, James 4:4). Enemies are in the opposite camp. I served as the regional attorney for a Texas state agency and had a friendly relationship with the other executives. One executive had violated a work rule, which led to his termination from his position. I was aware of the moment that his manager acted because I had to deem it a legally sufficient action before it could take place. After the executive was released, he immediately rushed to my office, presumably because we had a friendly relationship. I had to gingerly tell him if we ended up in court over the matter, I will be on the opposite side from him. Sin is what causes us to be on the opposite side from God. Without personal salvation, you are in the opposite camp from God. If saved, take care that you do not behave in such a manner that places you on the opposite side from God.

2. Evangelism

Unbelievers do not have a reconciled relationship with God. A minister of reconciliation has a responsibility to help others be reconciled to God. An old TV commercial related to helping those on drugs showed a drugged out person lying on a train track as a fast-moving train approached. A person on a bike watched for a while and then slowly and casually backed away his bike still watching the coming catastrophe without warning the person of danger. We do the same when we fail to lead others to Christ to bring them into the arc of safety.

Only when a person knows Christ can they best navigate diversity encounters, unresolved conflict, and other life issues. Help people come from enmity with God to peace with God through salvation.

> Then Jesus came to them and said, All authority in heaven and on earth has been given to me. Therefore go and make disciples of all nations, baptizing them in the name of the Father and of the Son and of the Holy Spirit, and teaching them to obey everything I have commanded you. And surely I am with you always, to the very end of the age (Matthew 18:18-20).

CONFLICT RESOLUTION MINISTRY OF RECONCILIATION

The Fall in the Garden of Eden not only gave us separation from God but separation from fellowman. Before the Fall man was at peace with God, others, and even animals. Because of Christ, we can restore our relationships with others. He mandates that we pursue peace and building up one another (see Romans 14:19). The ministry of reconciliation is not just about being reconciled to God, it is also about being reconciled to our brothers and sisters in Christ.

3. Resolving Personal Conflict with Others

God expects us to live reconciled lives by resolving conflict as a way of life. When we serve as ministers of reconciliation, we promote peace. Each peacemaking action is a witness of Christ in us. Christ is the minister of reconciliation between God and humanity. We can model after Christ who reconciled us to God, and we can now reconcile our relationships with others.

The knowledge of what Christ did on the cross to reconcile us to God, though we did not deserve it, can help us reconcile with others, though they might not deserve it. Serve without expecting anything in return. He calls us to peace and unity, even within our differences (see Ephesians 2:11-19). Live ongoing reconciled lives with others.

4. Helping Others Resolve Their Conflicts

The cross is what makes our ministry of reconciliation possible within us. Jesus took away our sins and enmity with God to bring us into right fellowship with Him. Now we can live reconciled lives and be active reconcilers to help others bring peace out of diversity and conflict. "Consequently, you are no longer foreigners and strangers, but fellow citizens with God's people and also members of his household" (Ephesians 2:19. An example of helping others resolve conflict is found in Acts 15:36-37 where Barnabas came to resolve a conflict between Paul and Mark. Helping others reconcile conflict does not mean that people will immediately reconcile or reconcile at all. However, we have a responsibility to help others resolve conflict. God created us for good works (see Ephesians 2:10). A ministry of reconciliation is good work. Your ministry of reconciliation may include being a mediator between those in conflict, coaching them, or correcting them like the apostle Paul. Paul knew there could be no genuine reconciliation without an acknowledgment of sinful behavior and repentance for sin. Both of Paul's letters to the Corinthians describe his somewhat conflicted relationship with them. Yet, he acted as a minister of reconciliation to help others resolve conflict issues. Paul further states in Philippians 2, "Do nothing out of selfish ambition or vain conceit. Rather, in humility value others above yourselves, not looking to your own interests but each of you to the interests of the others" (Philippians 2:3-4).

THE URGENCY TO RECONCILE

You may be reluctant to reconcile with someone you sinned against, but Scripture mandates it and shows the urgency of reconciliation. "Therefore, if you are offering your gift at the altar and there remember that your brother or sister has something against you, leave your gift there in front of the altar. First, go and be reconciled to them; then come and offer your gift" (Matthew 5:23-24). We tend to hesitate to go to another person regarding our wrongdoing, especially if it is a major conflict, but we are required to do so.

I have a statement that I often use, "Trust God for the consequences of your obedience to Him." Go be reconciled as God directs, and don't worry about the results. The results are God's business. God will give the outcome He chooses based on our obedient actions and the other person's response. We have a personal responsibility to pursue peace regardless of the other person's actions (see Romans 12:18). You are responsible to God for your actions; others are responsible to God for their actions.

We see the urgency that God places on reconciled relationships where Scripture tells us to leave the altar. Imagine being at the altar and remembering that your brother has something against you. You are to promptly get up, leave the altar, and first reconcile to your brother, and then after you have reconciled, you are free to return to the altar to offer your gift (see Matthew 5:25). Thus, God places more urgency to reconcile a conflicted relationship than worshiping at the altar. It is like God is saying, "don't come up in My face with sin on you" due to unresolved conflict with another.

Our failure to follow the mandate to reconcile with others is egregious because God spared us from His wrath by providing Jesus as the sacrifice for our sins to reconcile us to God. Likewise, we should reconcile with others. The clear mandate is that we are supposed to live ongoing peaceful, reconciled lives absent sinful conflict.

WHO GOES TO WHOM FIRST–THE OFFENDER OR THE OFFENDED?

So important is reconciliation that God covers all the bases, where neither party has an excuse not to pursue peace. When you read Matthew 18:15 along with Matthew 5:23-24, you discover the offended and the offender each have a responsibility to go. If you have sinned against someone, go (see Matthew 5:24). If someone has sinned against you, go (see Matthew 18:15). We will address this more specifically later in this book.

Our ministry of reconciliation duties should always be at play. What do you imagine the culture would see if every believer rushed to pursue peaceful relationship with other believers? I know people won't always get it right and may not be ready to make peace, but God does not excuse us from attempting to make peace with them. "If it is possible, as far as it depends on you, live at peace with everyone" (Romans 12:18).

MINISTRY OF RECONCILIATION WORKS BY LOVE

Believers are the church. The church is where reconciliation between all groups is supposed to occur regardless of status that the culture may recognize. It is a vision of the unity we will see between all groups in the Kingdom. In the second century's Greco-Roman culture, God's people demonstrated they lived radically different from how the pagans lived. In the second century church, even pagans marveled at the difference in the church with the statement: "See how they love one another."

Though the statement "See how they love one another" is not expressly in the Bible, it is an interpretation by an early church leader, Tertullian, related to how the early church put God's Word in action. He said that even pagans marveled at the love Christians showed one another. He wrote, "It is mainly the deeds of a love so noble that lead many to put a brand upon us. See how they love one another, they say, for they themselves are animated by mutual hatred; how they are ready even to die for one another (The Apology, Ch. 39). Because they showed love toward one another, their behavior reflected scriptural mandate. "By this shall all men know that you are my disciples if you have love one for another" (John 13:35). That is what we want the culture to see of us today. Our behavior, whether good or bad, is our reputation to the culture. Lovingly serving in your capacity as a minister of reconciliation despite differences is the approach God desires for us.

CHAPTER 5

RELATIONSHIPS AND SOCIAL INTERACTION MANAGEMENT

God made us for relationships, a relationship with
Him, and relationships with one another.

Life is about relationships. Satan's goal is to disrupt relationships and divide us, which he started with Adam and Eve. One of his primary ways to divide is through conflict. God uses people to bless us and for our growth. The devil uses people to disrupt us and try to destroy our lives. When we have conflict and division, we disinvite God from our circles. His essence is love, peace, and unity, as in the operation of the Godhead; oneness.

RELATIONSHIPS WORK BY LOVE

Not only does the ministry of reconciliation work by love, but love is God's nature and the theme that runs throughout the Bible. Outside of yourself, only two categories of relationship exist; (1) relationship with God, (2) relationship with others. Only when we have an appropriate relationship with God can we have the right relationship with ourself and others. Jesus gave evidence of relationship importance when He responded to a question regarding which is the greatest commandment.

> Jesus replied: "Love the Lord your God with all your heart and with all your soul and with all your mind. This is the first and greatest commandment. And the second is like it: Love your neighbor as yourself" (Matthew 22:37-39).

God's greatest commandments center around love. Love is central to and the pinnacle characteristic for relationships. Love is the connector that ties believers together (see Colossians 3:14). We are nothing without love (see 1 Corinthians 13). We prove love by our actions (see 1 John 3:18). Thus, the best approach for diverse counters is interact with love.

ORDERLY SOCIETAL INTERACTION

Diversity encounters involve others. We grow in Christian community. Christian community refers to our social interaction with others, not a physical location. Christian community contains people with a wealth of differences. God cares for the welfare of His people and wants us to have social well-being. You have likely heard the African proverb, "It takes a village to raise a child." The quote is a healthy outlook for the body of Christ, helping each other to live the Christian life. We need other people to apply biblical principles like love, the pursuit of peace, humility, gentleness, patience, and forgiveness to help us grow.

The Colossian church was out of order in how they related to one another. In Colossians 3, the apostle Paul provided direction for appropriate social interrelationships. The church at Colossae consisted of diverse groups, like churches and society today; various races, personalities, social status, etc. Paul lumps the diverse group into one basket, the body of Christ, with no other distinction. "Here there is no Gentile or Jew, circumcised or uncircumcised, barbarian, Scythian, slave or free, but Christ is all, and is in all" (Colossians 3:11). God calls us to peace and harmony within diversity for orderly living (see Colossians 3:15).

The fact that Paul was addressing believers tells us that believers do not always behave righteously. He reminded the Colossians that since identifying with Christ as Lord, they are responsible for living their lives according to the new life given to them by Christ. For orderly living, he instructed them to cease doing certain behaviors because they were acting contrary to God's will. He named sexual immorality, impurity, lust, evil desires, anger, rage, malice, slander, and filthy language (See Colossians 3:5, 3:8). Paul refers to unrighteous behavior as idolatry because they put unrighteous behavior before righteous behavior, meaning they put it before God. Anything we put before God is idolatry.

In Colossians 3:12, Paul used the metaphor of changing clothing and directed them to take off the unrighteous clothes and put on righteous garments of compassion, kindness, humility, gentleness, and patience. He gave specific instructions to bear with one another and forgive. "Bear with each other and forgive one another if any of you has a grievance against someone. Forgive as the Lord forgave you" (Colossians 3:13).

Paul's call for unity is a call for peace. In Hebrew, the word "shalom" means a complete sense or disposition of well-being or prosperity. When we live in peace, we meet God's plan for us to live orderly.

INTERRELATE BY SEPARATING THE PERSON FROM THEIR CONDUCT

In a nutshell, separating the person from their conduct helps in pursuing peace. It means to interrelate in diversity encounters appropriately, you should have proper regard for people as fellow image-bearers, show love, and separate the person from their behavior as specified in the below points to use in diversity encounters.

The Encounter: Recognize the encounter did not get to you, but that God allowed it; assigned it to you.

You: Embrace the ministry of reconciliation assignment. Decide to handle the encounter constructively, in a God-honoring way.

The Person: Don't have resentment toward the person. Immediately separate the person from their behavior that concerns you. The person is a fellow human made in God's image. Everyone matters, and everyone is valuable. Bear with the person. Treat the person with respect and dignity.

The Issue/Conduct: Determine whether the issue is a differing opinion or a sin issue that violates a biblical principle.

- If it is merely a differing perspective, allow for differences. Compromise where feasible.

- If it is a biblical principle at issue, hold fast. Do not violate God's standards. Embrace/accept the person; reject sinful conduct.

- Note that when we disrespect others made in God's image, we act beneath who we are in Christ and violate 1 Peter 2:17.

Be Mindful: Keep love in the forefront.

- Remember the two greatest commandments; love God with all your being and love others as yourself (see Matthew 22:38-39). All other commandments flow from and are summed up in the two greatest commandments. Love reflects the right heart attitude. Performing actions without love is legalism.

- "In essentials, unity; in non-essentials, liberty; in all things, charity" (St Augustine of Hippo).

PART 3

GOD USES UNCHANGEABLE DIFFERENCES TO GROW US

In this section we explore six unchangeable differences: spiritual gifts, personality, learning styles, race, generational, and gender.

CHAPTER 6

SPIRITUAL GIFTS

God gave us so much diversity that it is like He primed the pump for our growth. Various meanings for "prime the pump" exist, but all relate to doing something to make something else succeed. One example involves putting money in a tip jar at service locations for others to see the money to encourage them to give a real tip. Thus, the tip jar is primed for tips to flow. Another relates to government spending to stimulate the economy, which we periodically see in government stimulus packages designed for the people to spend money to stimulate economic growth.

The third analogy relates to the old archaic water pump, not the fancy ones of today with power, water hoses, and the like. At 3-4 years old, I watched my brothers prime an old water pump on our farm. They primed it by putting a small droplet of water into the pump, and then one of them would vigorously pump the handle. Voila! Water gushed out—fresh drinking water from an underground well. I marveled at the miracle water and never understood the mechanics of their answers when I questioned them about how the water did that. We may not fully understand the mechanics of spiritual life and how we can grow and unify from diverse encounters, but we can. Unlike a water pump, spiritual life is not mechanical but involves the heart.

Diversity encounters are a set up to grow up. The encounters expose our sin, which is good. Otherwise, we would not know to correct it.

Repentance from sinful handling of various encounters helps us grow and improve our relationships with God and others. As ministers of reconciliation, we operate to maintain peace.

If we prime the pump by dropping the right behavior into a situation and vigorously pump the handle of righteous action, peace and unity more likely flow. On the other hand, if we prime the pump with sinful behavior and vigorously pump the handle, then division and strife flow from the encounter. Sometimes conflicts are small, and sometimes they are gushers, depending on the nature of the dispute and the behavior of those involved. The bigger the battle, the more significant stride of spiritual growth when we apply biblical principles. Our vast differences provide us built-in situations for good or bad based on how we handle them. Diversity is part of God's universal plan. We either pump the sinful handle or the righteousness handle. Only one of those leads us to unity and harmony desired by God.

Let's take a sightseeing tour of our multitude of unchangeable differences that we can embrace to help us grow and unify. I start with spiritual gifts as my first primed pump because the gifts directly illustrate that God gave diversity of gifts to spiritually mature the church and unify the church (see 1 Corinthians 12).

Spiritual gifts are assigned to believers at the point of salvation and are supernatural endowments to every believer for the benefit of the body of Christ, the church. The spiritual gifts show we need each other since no one is given all the gifts. When we recognize that we need each other, prudence dictates we unify. The Bible expresses our triune God's oneness; three persons in one Godhead—Father, Son, and Holy Spirit. We are one body in Christ, and Jesus prays that we may be one as He is one with the Father. "That all of them may be one, Father, just as you are in me and I am in you. May they also be in us so that the world may believe that you have sent me" (John 17:21). Members of God's body constitute the whole, and each part is needed. The theme of unity and oneness run throughout the Bible. Oneness comes with spiritual growth and brings unity within diversity.

Scripture tells us that the Spirit gives us varying gifts, but one Spirit, one Lord, and one Father (see 1 Corinthians 12). In each verse of 1 Corinthians 12:4-6, the word "differences" is mentioned related to spiritual gifts. "There are different kinds of gifts, but the same Spirit distributes them. There are different kinds of service, but the same LORD. There are different kinds of working, but in all of them and in everyone it is the same God at work" (1 Corinthians 12:6). Scripture further explains why the spiritual gifts are given—for our common good (see 1 Corinthians 12:7). One God works in each of us. His law is unity. Since the body is one and the gifts are given to unify us, how then can we have so much conflict related to our differences? We allow our differences to lead to conflict, contrary to unity within our diversity described in 1 Corinthians 12.

UNHEALTHY COMPETITION

The apostle Paul encouraged unity, not fighting regarding who is the best leader. "What I mean is this: One of you says, 'I follow Paul; another, I follow Apollos; another, I follow Cephas; still another, I follow Christ'" (1 Corinthians 1:12). In the following verse, Paul shared that Christ is not divided, (see Romans 1:13). We esteem and lift up various people, but no human took away sin, only Christ did or could take away sin. For peace and unity, we keep the focus on Christ. Otherwise, we head into division and strife.

Disunity can come from unhealthy competition and ugly jealousies related to others' spiritual gifts; preacher, teacher, giver, leader, or other endowments. We are not competitors, but fellow laborers. It is nonsensical to have jealousy regarding another's gift when none of us bestowed gifts upon ourselves. The Holy Spirit provides each person with gifts for the building up of the body and to unify the body. When you focus on another person's gifts, you miss the blessing of the gifts God gave you. We need all the spiritual gifts of everyone. Note that God did not give any one person all of the spiritual gifts, which I believe is a set up for us to need each other.

Scripture uses an anatomical analogy to illustrate how we need the varying gifts for unity. It says the foot can't say of the hand I don't need you or the ear to the eye, I don't need you (see 1 Corinthians 12:15-26).

God made each to be part of the whole body. Each is necessary for the entire body to function at its optimum. A pastor without members does not make a local church.; nor does a teacher without students make a Sunday School class; nor does a music leader without singers make a choir.

God did not give us gifts to lift our egos in pride but for us to contribute to the body's needs. We can enjoy using our gifts, but He gave them for the benefit of the corporate body. People needing others and unifying is like the beauty of an orchestra of varying instruments that fall pleasurably on the ear. "How good and pleasant it is when God's people live together in unity" (Psalm 133:1).

God uses spiritual gifts and the spiritually gifted to grow us individually and corporately. Ephesians 4 also directly expresses both points. Differing gifts are provided to mature and unify the church.

> So Christ himself gave the apostles, the prophets, the evangelists, the pastors and teachers, to equip his people for works of service, so that the body of Christ may be built up until we all reach unity in the faith and in the knowledge of the Son of God and become mature, attaining to the whole measure of the fullness of Christ (Ephesians 4:11-13).

Through lack of knowledge and pride, we inappropriately compete because we desire to bring glory to ourselves rather than bring glory to God and build up the body of Christ, contrary to Scripture. In Philippians, Paul exhorts the church to do nothing out of rivalry or envy (see Philippians 2:3). Glory belongs only to God. "Not to us, LORD, not to us but to your name be the glory, because of your love and faithfulness" (Psalm 115:1). When we raise ourselves up, the opposite happens to us; we go down. "Pride goes before destruction, a haughty spirit before a fall" (Proverbs 16:18). If we want to be great, then serve others. "The greatest among you will be your servant. For those who exalt themselves will be humbled, and those who humble themselves will be exalted" (Matthew 23:11-12).

Bill Lawrence, former Dallas Theological Seminary professor taught about the "Dreaded Leaders Disease." It is when someone pursues their interest in Jesus's name. God blesses us with spiritual gifts so we can bless others. We are to encourage and support one another's ministries, not compete with them. We grow and unify when we apply biblical principles. Unhealthy competition brings evil. "For where you have envy and selfish ambition, there you find disorder and every evil practice" (James 3:16).

When we remove pride and humble ourselves, we see the truth of ourselves as small and needing God, which gives us the right perspective to manage diverse encounters. The Holy Spirit provides us with the power to forbear and love. Love is the adhesive that unites us in peace. If we push against God, His refiner's fire gets hotter to get sinful impurities out of us. Any fight with God is futile. He always wins. It is His world, wherein He designed diversity to make us holy more than merely because He loves diversity.

CHAPTER 7

PERSONALITY

W e have all likely heard of personality clashes. God bestows spiritual gifts at the point of salvation, whereas our personalities come at birth. We see personalities early in babies. Based on personality type, we have a predictable pattern of behavior, referred to as personality temperaments. Encounters with diverse temperaments can lead to conflict.

Encounters with diverse temperaments are an excellent place to grow and learn to unite. Recall that our goal is unity, and we use the theme that God designed diversity to help us grow so we can learn to operate in peace and harmony. That does not mean we should try to be the same as others, but we can have unity within diversity, as shared in the chapter on spiritual gifts.

We often engage in conflict because we do not understand our differences and do not allow for others' differences. As we grow through the encounters and spiritually mature, we learn to obey the commandments to love and pursue peace with one another. Since God loves diversity, why would we hate what God loves?

Think about your family members, friends, church leaders, and people at work. Note all the different personalities. Personality differences are typical, yet people want others to change their personalities. If we desire another person to be more like us, we want to countermand traits God created in them. We can neither change our personalities or

anyone else's. Though we cannot change our basic personality temperament, we can submit our natural personality temperaments to conform to God's standards.

Without recognizing differences in God-given personal wiring,
husbands and wives try to change their mate's personality to be like
theirs. Parents crush what God naturally gave the child when they try
to force the child to do it the way the parent would do it or how a sib-
ling would do it. It causes frustration, conflict, and rebellion. I do not
speak of correcting a child's wrongful behavior but speak against sti-
fling a child's natural temperament, like forcing a naturally gregarious
child to become subdued. It kills their spirit. When you hear people say,
I would do it another way, it is because God wired them another way.
No one can do it someone else's way, because God made them differently. When we do not allow for differences in personalities, misunderstanding, resentment, and discouragement result and lead to conflict.
When we allow for differences, it leads to peace.

In conflict resolution classes, I sometimes ask students if they
believe they are valuable. All hands go up. I then ask if other people
are valuable. Some hesitantly raise their hand, and some keep down
their hand, to which the class chuckles. Valuables. I have a few valuable
items that belonged to my mom before she went home to be with the
Lord. Those items are mostly valuable to me because it reminds me of
the love between a mother and daughter. I treat those valuables with
care. Most people treat their valuables with care.

What makes people valuable? In *The Search for Significance*, Robert McGee tells us that we are valuable because God created us in His
image.[2] In addition, the fact that Christ died for us is further evidence
of our value. You do not die for something worthless. Our value never
changes. It is intrinsic and not based on performance or feelings. People are more valuable than the most valuable item we own. However,
people can act beneath their value.

The world is made up of valuable people with diverse personalities, which can collide. When we recognize people as valuable, we
will more likely treat them with the respect and dignity they deserve
as humanity, which includes allowing for differences. When we treat

people as valuable, it meets a basic human need and generally brings a positive result. Abraham Maslow's hierarchy of needs shows the need for esteem as one of our greatest human needs. Respecting and valuing people meets that need and curtails conflict. It helps us grow and brings more peace and unity.

There are no bad personalities but bad behavior. The core issue for believers is not the personality itself but bringing the personality temperament under submission to God for righteous behavior. Psychologist William Marston was the first to introduce the DISC personality model of human temperament, based on Hippocrates' defining work. The DISC acronym represents the personality traits, Dominant (D), Influence (I), Steadiness (S) and Conscientious (C). A better understanding of basic personality temperaments and behavioral patterns can help us during diversity encounters.

Our personality explains why we do what we do. God made all personalities to benefit us. When we feel downcast, we can benefit more from a supportive "S" personality than a critical "C" personality. When we are sinful, we need a critical "C" personality who is motivated by correctness. However, the critical "C" personality needs to speak the truth in love instead of the natural tear-down spirit. Many strong leaders have "D" personalities who take charge and control. There are times and places that we need the "D" personality, analogous to the Analytic general to make military decisions in battle, referred to in chapter 1. We have all seen the "I" personality, who is the life of the party to lighten up things.

Businesses recognize the benefit of interdisciplinary teams of diverse perspectives for more creativity and better production. Like in a multidisciplinary group with various skills, all temperaments can benefit if we avoid personality collisions and accept differences. When we learn to interact with different personalities, we become more inclined toward God's goal of oneness in His family of believers. Recall the "diversity rub" definition in chapter 2. *Diversity rub* is sinful intolerance of others and their differences. It can produce friction or conflict if we interact sinfully, which is tied to intolerance of others and their differences. On the other hand, when we interact in a God-honoring manner, peace more likely results. When we grow from the encounter, we keep peace.

A common analogy for growth is the metamorphosis struggle that the caterpillar goes through to become a butterfly. It parallels our spiritual growth of learning to work with different personalities. After the caterpillar goes through the struggle in the cocoon, the ugly worm turns into a beautiful butterfly that comes out and gracefully flies away. We are unattractive like the worm in the cocoon until we transform from low-ground behavior to lovely flight. When we learn to work with and accept others' differences, our transformation takes us from our unlovely character to Christlike persona. We can then fly higher in interactions by forbearing, forgiving, and loving one another. You will never see a butterfly attempt to go back into the dead shell cocoon that it left behind. Not so with humans.

Have you noticed how groups also have personalities? One teacher talked about a particular third-grade class whose personalities combined such that no one wanted to teach that rough little band. They remained together as a class and had the same reputation from third grade until they graduated from elementary school. Regarding a particular work team, people said they had noticed the peaceful work environment since X left the company.

I taught the personality DISC to a small adult class. Interestingly, all of them tested as "D" personalities. The "D" is the controlling personality. I thought, these people will wrestle this class right out of my hands if I am not careful. However, it made for excellent class interaction. I also taught a small class where the students were primarily of the "S" supportive personality. They were pleasant to teach but did not have as much stimulating conversation. Another class of mainly "I" personalities (life of the party) was full of fun. At the first class, within minutes of arrival, I noted they were a vibrant group. Laughter at each other frequently erupted. I had to periodically pull them from jokes to the seriousness of the class.

I have never experienced a primarily "C" personality class, the critical group. I imagine a class with many "C" critical personality types could be a drain to teach but would help you grow as a teacher. I prefer a mixture of all personalities in classes, but whatever the dynamics, it is advisable to use Paul's wisdom, who conformed himself to others' feelings that he might save some. "To the weak I became weak, to win the weak. I have become all things to all people so that by all possible means I might save some" (1 Corinthians 9:22). We cannot change our basic temperament, but we can control it and apply biblical principles to interact with others harmoniously, whether individually or in a group. Working with the diverse personality groups helped me grow as a teacher and believer.

God is looking to see Christ's character in our hearts, including how we treat people with whom we differ. Learn to accept others' differences. "If a Man Answers" is a movie from the early 70s starring Sandra Dee and Bobby Darren, who played a young married couple. Sandra Dee's character received guidance from her mom on how to have a happy marriage. Her mom told her to use the principles in a book related to how to train your dog. She used the dog training principles on her husband, and it worked! Sandra Dee would report back to her mom periodically, only to realize in the end that it was not her husband who had changed, but she had changed in her perspective and behavior toward him. When you change your outlook, you can then look out and see a better view of others, despite personality differences.

People can sometimes rub you the wrong way. One person in particular comes to mind. When I talk to her on the phone, and she goes into her critical mode, I have a game I play with myself. I smile, point at the phone, and silently mouth the word "valuable" to remind me she is a valuable person made in God's image. Thus far, it has worked, but she has not changed her behavior. I changed my outlook. Now, I more clearly see where the person has much to offer that I previously missed due to intolerance. I have learned much from her and continue to do so. It helps when we become more God-focused and less self-focused. British theologian Lesslie Newbigin says it excellently:

> History is to be understood as the patient wrestling of God
> with a stupid, deluded, and rebellious people—stupid and

rebellious precisely because they insist on seeing themselves as the center of the story.[3]

The apostle Paul's analogy of being all things to all people can help salespeople make a sale. I provide two examples: (1) If you try to make a sale to a "D" personality, be direct and go bottom line to close the deal. The "D" personality wants you to get to the point. (2) If you are trying to sell to an "S" personality, don't try to close the deal too fast; they won't go for it. It would help if you drew them out. The same analogy applies to diverse temperament encounters. Allowing for differences in personalities enables us to win people and live more harmoniously with them. God knows what He is doing. We need the different personalities from which we learn to interact with humility for spiritual growth and unity. We can open our hearts, broaden our minds, and increase our knowledge and experiences to enjoy all that God created. We can interact peacefully and unify within His created diversity for His glory.

BIBLICAL EXAMPLES OF DIFFERING PERSONALITIES

Abraham's wife Sarah showed her high "D" controlling personality in Genesis 16. She was unable to have a child, but took control of the situation by persuading Abraham to sleep with her maid Hagar to get a child. Her controlling temperament is further demonstrated when she demanded that Abraham throw out the handmaid who became arrogant after she produced Abraham's heir, Ishmael. Though it pained Abraham to do so because of Ishmael, he demonstrated his "S" supportive personality by complying with Sarah's demands.

The high "I" influencer or people person, likes to be accepted by people and does not like rejection. In 1 Samuel 15, we see Saul disobey God and let the people pressure him to take bounty after the destruction of Amalek contrary to God's instructions. Moses revealed his "C" personality in his writing the books of the law with precision and accuracy.

CHAPTER 8

LEARNING STYLE DIFFERENCES

I n chapter 1, I talked about learning styles where we used Bernice McCarthy's categories because of the concrete example from the classroom exercise. That exercise reinforced the principle to allow for others' differences. Bloom's Taxonomy is another learning style. It shows how different learning styles have skills that come together for teamwork. I add it here because of known characters you might recognize and readily see the differences. Some believe the Star Trek series writer developed his characters from Bloom's Taxonomy.

BLOOM'S TAXONOMY

Bloom's Taxonomy describes learning style differences as (1) Affective, (2) Cognitive, and (3) Psychomotor domains of learning. The Affective domain learner learns best in a pleasant environment where they "feel" safe. The Cognitive domain learner learns best where the teaching causes them to "think." The Psychomotor domain learner learns best in an environment where they "do" through a learning activity related to the teaching point. In *Created to Learn*, William R. Yount analyzes Bloom's three domains to the four key Star Trek characters. Yount believes that the Star Trek creator, Gene Roddenberry, was familiar with Bloom's domains because Star Trek's characters fit the domains perfectly.

Cognitive Domain—In the Star Trek series, Lt. Commander Spock was half human and half Vulcan. He personified the Cognitive domain. Spock suppressed his human self and focused on the rational Vulcan self. He is a thinker, a cerebral, brilliant being who focuses on the rational, informational, factual aspect. Jobs that rely heavily on facts and data need the Spock types of the world. They learn best in the traditional classroom and can hear nuanced information in lectures that other learners often miss. This type can also engender conflict by not being as relatable to people. We grow when we learn to allow for lack of interpersonal relationships skills in some. Doing so also helps us keep the peace.

Affective Domain—Doctor "Bones" McCoy models the Affective domain because he is all emotion and reacts based on his feelings. He is a walking, talking Affective domain. He handled medical problems well but wore his emotions on his sleeve. His relationships with people involved emotional outbursts that flew everywhere, from anger to joy, love, happiness, frustration, and impatience. We note that teaming a Cognitive (Spock) and an Affective (Bones) pair for a job project or other interaction can result in conflict if they do not allow for others' differences. Affective domain learners need an emotionally supportive learning environment. For peace, they need to use the apostle Paul's "be all things to all people." Paul had complete freedom, yet he adapted for the sake of saving others.

> Though I am free and belong to no one, I have made myself a slave to everyone, to win as many as possible. To the Jews I became like a Jew, to win the Jews. To those under the law I became like one under the law (though I myself am not under the law), so as to win those under the law. To those not having the law I became like one not having the law (though I am not free from God's law but am under

Christ's law), so as to win those not having the law. To the weak I became weak, to win the weak. I have become all things to all people so that by all possible means I might save some. I do all this for the sake of the gospel, that I may share in its blessings (1 Corinthians 9:19-23).

Like the apostle Paul, we can learn to encourage and give emotional support for a higher goal than self-focus. We can learn to bear with others and accept differences for peace and unity.

Psychomotor Domain—We see the Psychomotor domain in Chief Engineer Scottie, who is a technical mastermind. His brilliance keeps the starship Enterprise operational. He is the "get it done" person. His mastermind allows him to coordinate starship systems to accomplish things not considered in the starship design. He personifies the Psychomotor domain, the doers. They learn best by doing learning exercises associated with the teaching points. Recognize and accept this different style for peace and harmony.

Cognitive/Affective/Psychomotor Domains—We see a balance of all the domains in Captain James T. Kirk. He can be rational like Spock, have feelings like Bones, and do things like Scottie. As was often shown in the series, Bones (Affective) and Spock (Cognitive) were the protagonists. Spock detested Bones's irrational emotions, and Bones hated Spock's lack of emotion. They often fought and engaged in conflict, yet the starship Enterprise needed all of them for successful operations. They carried out their duties but did not know how to relate to each other appropriately and were intolerant of differences. Although Star Trek was fictional, Yount's analogy illustrates my point. We are better together and need the differences. God designed us for unity. Embrace differences, learn, and grow.

I had a student in a conflict resolution training course who was an Affective domain learner who needed encouragement and support. He also appeared to have learning struggles, which I later learned was his unusual communication style. The other students were astonished by his questions that did not seem to make sense. During a class session, he asked a question that rang out as a dumb question. I did not say that he asked a dumb question. It sounded like what people would say is a dumb question because it seemed nonsensical. The entire class laughed at the question. At their laugher, I became keenly aware that I was teaching conflict resolution and wanted to model what I was teaching. I knew I had to model treating the student with respect and dignity. I treated the student respectfully knowing the other students watched to see how I would handle the matter.

I did not understand the student's question. I kept a straight face and decided to ask him a series of open-ended questions to understand better. It took about 3-4 questions for me to pull out of him what he was asking. When I finally understood what he was asking, it was a great question, and I answered it. After I responded to the question, to my great amazement, the student immediately brightened and said these words: "This is the best day of my life!" From that moment to the end of the semester, his whole countenance changed, as did his treatment by other class members. They no longer looked at him with ridicule.

From that one episode, God taught me that there are no dumb questions from students. The students are there to learn. While there are no dumb students, there can be dumb teachers who do not appropriately respond to students. Differences. That was a learning episode for me to realize the importance of allowing for differences. Even now, I marvel at how something seemingly insignificant could change a student's countenance the remainder of the semester, and also change the other students' attitude toward him. When we thoughtlessly ridicule others, it affects them, as it would also affect us. People have feelings and emotions. People matter. My respecting and allowing for the student's difference helped me grow as a teacher and taught the other students by example to allow for differences. The class became more unified.

I have not always had wisdom in interactions but have learned from experience and observing good and bad examples. The bad examples teach you what not to do. I attended conflict resolution training many years ago and came back to the class early after a 10-minute break. I caught the two teachers arguing about which of them was the lead trainer in charge of the training. It struck me that they were not practicing what they were teaching. They modeled it poorly. I never forgot that lesson, especially when I teach conflict resolution. I recalled it with the student's question, so I was extra careful with my response and to model it. You too can model it and impact yourself and others.

God gave us a multitude of differences that can bring naturally arising circumstances for us to take advantage of by applying biblical principles to model the right behavior to grow therefrom.

CHAPTER 9

RACE

R ace is one of many differences that people allow to lead to sinful conflict instead of embracing it as desired by God. A poem I wrote in 2019 titled "Differences" sheds some light on the race issue.

Differences
(Colossians 3:13; 1 Corinthians 10:31)

God did not make us alike in appearance, personalities, or gifts
He had a plan in mind, elevated far above our petty tiffs.

Our differences can lead to much conflict
If we do not allow the Holy Spirit to convict.

In His handiwork, we see God loves diversity.
Sadly, some use it for division and adversity.

When we don't practice differences sensitivity,
We're an ungodly example for the world to see.

Embracing differences is embracing God.
All made in His image, on this earth we trod.

Living souls in different colors, hues and tones.
Yet, in every shade, His breath of life is blown.

Bearing with one another, loving, and forgiving
Is what He tells us we need for righteous living.

Take the opportunity to practice unity within our diversity.
Be a personal beacon of light for our dark world to see.

The chief aim of life should be to bring Him glory.
When it's all said and done, what will be your story?

When you explore the magnitude of the race issue, you realize it's like an onion. As you peel one layer, another shows itself. Psychologists say that our perspectives and interactions about race come from learned behavior.

NO LESSER IMAGE

Scripture is sufficient to educate us regarding the race issue. God created man in His image (see Genesis 1:26-27). Man is the only being that God personally breathes life into. "Then the LORD God formed a man from the dust of the ground and breathed into his nostrils the breath of life, and the man became a living being" (Genesis 2:7). God did not create a lesser or inferior image bearer, but He did make the other animals inferior to man. We are made in God's image in terms of our will, intellect, and emotion.

God named the man Adam, which is Hebrew for "man-kind." It represents generic man without racial connotation. All other humans came from Adam. "From one man he made all the nations, that they should inhabit the whole earth; and he marked out their appointed times in history and the boundaries of their lands" (Acts 17:26).

In a book club of diverse races, we read John Piper's *Bloodlines*. When I mentioned we all came from one man, one woman of another race became visibly upset and said, everyone does not agree. I don't argue with people who disagree with the Bible, especially when they are visibly upset. However, I marveled that she is a Christian and took issue with the Bible, so deep was her perception of race. She reminded me of a woman at my former church who was in a heated argument with a deacon. When he told her what the Bible said about the issue, she yelled, "I don't care what the Bible says." He said we can't go further until we deal with the statement you just made. She then looked embarrassed and said she didn't mean that. We generally mean what we say when we say it.

Race is one of the many differences God made that, when properly responded to, brings growth and unity. If the universal church comprised of all believers everywhere came together regarding the racial divide, we would see God respond in amazing ways. I touch primarily the black/white issue in this chapter as representative of others since it often appears to lead to the most division. I remind you of the definition of diversity embrace from chapter 2. *Diversity embrace is* godly tolerance of others and their differences. God requires us to bear with one another and allow for others' differences (see Colossians 3:13, Ephesians 4:2). Some Christians close their hearts to truth based on deep-rooted learned fallacy regarding race. Both the Colossians and Ephesians passages speak of bearing with one another, loving, and forgiving. I do not speak of tolerating sin but tolerance of others differences. However, even in the case of sin, the Bible instructs us to love the sinner, not sinful behavior.

None of *Diversity of a Different Kind* will work without submission to God. Like other diversity encounters, our racial diversity encounters can expose sin within. Recall from our Ministry of Reconciliation chapter, we are each commissioned by Christ as ministers of reconciliation to help reconcile others to Christ and help them reconcile conflicted relationships. Race is not excluded. As ministers of reconciliation, we please and honor God when we embrace people of different races for our optimum spiritual well-being.

RACIAL CATEGORIES CONCEPT

God made humans in His image. He breathed His DNA and breath into us. We are the same in our humanity. It boggles my mind when I think that the very breath I breathe is God's breath in me. As walking, talking, God-breathers, we can have unity within diversity without losing the beauty of God's creative diversity. However, man categorizes us into three groups of people: Caucasoid, Mongoloid, and Negroid.

Shiao Chong's article "Racism, Revelation and Recipes: Towards Christian Inter-Cultural Communities" provides his perspective on ethnic diversity and racism, part of which I quote here.

> Race is an artificial pseudo-scientific category used to describe people who share biologically transmitted traits …what is even more important is that these rather insignificant physical traits are given social significance by ideology. These physical "racial" traits only have social significance because we give them significance—they are artificial. We are accustomed to think that these physical differences amount to some moral and social differences such as intelligence, goodness, beauty, honesty… Such thinking is rooted in a distorted ideology, not in creation. Because this idolatrous ideology is systemic in our culture, it has affected all of us.[4]

Race only has significance because we give it significance. Chong describes it as being caught in a web of systemic racism. I saw a Twilight Zone film once that stuck with me. A lady had undergone her eleventh facial surgery to look normal like others. Throughout the program, we only saw her bandaged face and heard how ugly she looked from her doctors and nurses, whose faces were also not shown. The medical staff was concerned about whether the surgery had worked. The woman was anxious to have the bandages removed to see if they had changed her appearance.

The doctor removed her bandages, and with disappointment, he announced that the surgery had failed. It was then that the camera showed the woman's face, which by our cultural standard would be considered beautiful. The camera then cut to the faces of the medical staff who were deemed to be beautiful in that society. The medical team had sunken eyes, pigs' snouts, and twisted lips, which we would consider to be grotesque.[5] Because the surgery was so unsuccessful, a man came and took the woman away to a village where people looked like her. The doctor pronounced what does it matter, "beauty is in the eyes of the beholder."[6] Many people get braces to eliminate space between teeth. I read an article titled "There is beauty in a gap-tooth![7] In some countries, the gap-tooth is considered beautiful. We allow societal norms to tell us what is beautiful. God created diversity of looks, and it is all good, whether it is thick lips, thin lips, kinky hair, straight hair, slanted eyes, oval or round eyes. Humanity is God's specially designed diversity, all beautiful. However, beauty fades. Those who honor God are the true beauties.

Our true character does not consist of our physical appearance, but what is in our hearts. God judges us based on what is in our hearts. The prophet Samuel thought that Jesse's son Eliab would be God's chosen as the king because of his appearance. That was not the case. Our perspectives can be shallow. "But the LORD said to Samuel, 'Do not consider his appearance or his height, for I have rejected him. The LORD does not look at the things people look at. People look at the outward appearance, but the LORD looks at the heart'" (1 Samuel 16:7).

CALL TO ONENESS

We have a common enemy, who we do not physically see, other than in evil conduct when people act on his behalf. God made diversity and unity to coexist in harmony as in the Godhead; three distinct Persons in one; Father, Son, and Holy Spirit. Our ministries of reconciliation that God gives us include racial reconciliation. When we let our ethnic identity define us over our spiritual identity in Christ and act accordingly, we sin. God is not a respecter of persons based on race, class, or otherwise, nor should we be. "There is neither Jew nor Greek, slave nor free, male nor female, for you are all one in Christ Jesus" (Galatians 3:28). A time will come when God judges each of us, not based on our race, but on our conduct on earth (see Revelation 7:9).

God called us to oneness and unity across all races. We exist better united than divided. Look at the dramatic ushering in of God's pronouncement of no separation for His people. In the Old Testament, the high priests represented the people before God. They were responsible for making sacrifices to God for the sins of the people. The outer wall of the temple separated the Gentiles from the Jews. The penalty for a Gentile going beyond the exterior wall was death. The temple had two curtains. One that was in front of the Holy Place and one in front of the Holy of Holies. The Holy Place separated the Jewish people from the Holy of Holies. Only the High priest could enter the Holy of Holies, which housed the Ark of the Covenant and the Mercy Seat. He entered once a year on the Day of Atonement to atone for the sins of the people. Regular priests served in the Holy Place and made ritual sacrifices for people to approach God for sins committed after the Day of Atonement. The system separated Gentiles from the Jews and separated both groups from God.

Picture the description of powerful events surrounding Jesus's breaking down the separation walls to bring reconciliation. It turned dark during Christ's crucifixion, where daytime resembled night for 3 hours in the middle of the day. It was like saying, pay attention. This phenomenon of night in the middle of the day tells you something huge is happening. To me, that seems like a prelude to the coming attraction of events about to take place. At the moment when Jesus cried with a loud voice and breathed His last breath, the curtain in the temple that separated the groups ripped from top to bottom. A worldwide earthquake occurred. Rocks split, tombs broke open, and dead people came out of the grave and walked about. Thus, at Jesus's last breath, God dramatically ushered in the New Covenant with physical events that loudly pronounced Christ's finished work. It happened for all of us. Jesus took the sins of the whole world on Himself on the cross.

Through Christ's shed blood (no more animal sacrifices), He took the punishment we deserved for our sins and made possible our right standing with God. The torn curtain signifies there is no longer a separation between groups. Under the New Covenant, Jesus is our Superior High Priest, unlike Old Testament priests, where people continually needed repeated animal sacrifices. Jesus's sacrifice was once and for all.

IMPACT OF EXPERIENCES AND LEARNED BEHAVIOR

Many intellectually know that everyone is the same in God's eyes, but their behavior says they believe otherwise. Some of our perspectives are not based on God's truth but on experience and learned behavior. Countee Cullen's poem, "Incident," shows how life events can impact us at a young age and possibly for a lifetime and set in place a mentality of separateness over unity. "Incident" is a short poem that talks about the experience of a child who was happily touring Baltimore when he encountered another child who was very small like him. He smiled at the other child, who responded with a racial slur. The first child saw all of Baltimore during his visit, but the only thing he remembered over time was that one incident.

What incidents have you experienced or learned that influenced your perspective regarding other races that foster negative thinking and division? No one can take credit or discredit for the race God chose for us. We cannot change the face of our race, but we can change our attitudes during conflicts we face. "We must live together as brothers or perish together as fools" (Martin Luther King Jr.).

We put down the perspectives of others with different racial experiences. Many of us are ignorant about other races, yet full of clueless opinions. Some even take cues about racial issues from social media. We live in silos of communities like us and invalidate or contradict others' legitimate perspectives due to a lack of knowledge. Views can change as we educate ourselves that the world is more significant than our little spots in life.

THE BRAIN AND RACISM

Psychologist Steve Taylor, PhD, who has written 13 books on psychology and spirituality, states that racism is a sign of a lack of psychological maturity and integration.[8] He describes it as a defense mechanism to help feelings of insignificance. Racists treat members of their group well but treat others with hostility in order to foster a sense of identity in themselves. To the racist, other groups become scapegoats on which to project their own flaws. Like many others, Taylor describes race and racial categories:

> It is also helpful to remember that there is no biological basis for dividing the human race into distinct "races." There are just groups of human beings—all of whom came from Africa originally—who developed slightly different physical characteristics over time as they traveled to, and adapted to, different climates and environments. The differences between us are very fuzzy and very superficial. Fundamentally, there are no races—just one human race.

Cognitive neuroscientist, Bobby Azarian, PhD, states that although most people will say they have no racial bias, psychological experiments prove otherwise. Such experiments show negative connotations associated with the black face. "These troubling findings suggest that over 75% of Whites and Asians have an implicit racial bias, which affects how they process information and perceive the social world around them period.[9] Dr. Azarian says these biases are acted upon because they don't have a healthy prefrontal cortex of the brain, which helps control emotions. He speaks of rewiring the brain based on new stimuli. Scripture refers to it as renewing your mind with God's Word. "Do not conform to the pattern of this world, but be transformed by the renewing of your mind. Then you will be able to test and approve what God's will is—his good, pleasing and perfect will" (Romans 12:2).

INSIGHT FROM PERSONAL EXPERIENCES

A business associate and I were on a business trip in Severna Park, Maryland, when I realized that I was driving on the right street but going in the wrong direction to get to our destination. There was no other traffic, so I made a U-turn in the street and headed in the right direction. The friend who was riding with me frowned and said in an irritated voice, "What is wrong with you?" I looked at her, puzzled. She then asked why I had not just gone into a driveway to turn around instead of making a U-turn in the street. I made the U-turn action based on my subconscious data. I did not even realize what I had done. Upon hearing the question, the reason that I made the U-turn immediately floated up from my subconscious mind to my conscious awareness. I abruptly realized that I was in a box of which I was unaware. There I sat whole and complete in Christ, accepting all my freedom and grace in Him. Yet, there was a belief from a seed planted when I was a child that took root and loomed large in my subconscious. When I was a child, I heard, do not turn around in the driveway of a white person. They will shoot you. I am black. My friend is white. The only other time that I publicly shared the story was at a speaking engagement of 99% white people at a church regarding differences. When I made the statement about being shot, the room of people loudly gasped. We do not all have the same American experiences.

After the driving episode in Maryland, I phoned other black friends to ascertain if they had been told the same thing as children. The majority said they learned the same thing during childhood. From where do your assumptions about the races come? How did it foster separation of races? God reconciled racially divided groups into one (Ephesians 2:14-15) so that the church can function in unity (Ephesians 4:13). The church is where race, gender, and class distinctions are no longer supposed to divide us because of our unity in Christ. This is the issue that existed in the church of Galatia that Paul addressed: "There is neither Jew nor Gentile, neither slave nor free, nor is there male and female, for you are all one in Christ Jesus" (Galatians 3:28). Yet, we continue to see classism, sexism, and racism today, oftentimes unaddressed.

My Severna Park driving incident led me to a great interest in the psyche's impact on how we interact based on race. For my exploration of racial issues, I interviewed people of different races. One white woman shared that she was taught as a child that whites are better than blacks. Her information helps me understand some behavior. There are probably things in the subconscious and conscious mind of all of us on which we act on without thought. Some of these actions dishonor God. Our experiences should not lead us to invalidate or lack sensitivity for the feelings, positions, and experiences of others. Our diversity encounters can help us grow. We do not benefit from sinful intolerance due to a person's race. The harvest is full for healing the racial divide. Where are the ministry of reconciliation laborers?

Our experiences differ. On March 5, 2020, less than two months after Amanda Gorman recited her poem at the Joe Biden presidential inauguration, she posted on Twitter @TheAmandaGorman. "A security guard trailed me on my walk home tonight. He demanded if I lived there 'because I looked suspicious.' I showed my keys & buzzed myself into my building. He left, no apology. This is the reality of black girls: one day you're called an icon, the next day a threat."

It is possible the security guard acted from conditioning based on learned behavior and societal norms. I went through management training at a bank right out of college. I had to work in every department of the bank to learn the banking industry. As I observed at a teller's window, I asked the teller why she only did extra questioning of black customers and asked for their drivers' license, but not others. I believe today, banks generally ask for the identification of everyone. That was not the case then, but my point is, the teller treated black customers differently. In response to my question, she said the teller supervisor trained her to check black customers more closely. I later asked the teller supervisor. She said senior management told her to check blacks extra closely. Young me; I asked senior management but did not get an answer.

I am sure what management taught tellers consciously and subconsciously gave negative connotation of blacks. I remembered the teller incident years later when I was at a different bank after moving to another city. The teller called a supervisor, gave her my driver's license, and pointed to a name on a document she held that I could see (before technology prevalence). She pointed to a name, "Olga" Barnett. My license clearly showed "Oletha" Barnett. The supervisor said it is a different name, and she cashed my check. Whether right or not, because of my memory of the incident that occurred years earlier, I felt "extra checked."

BIASES AND VICTIMS

People can carry emotional baggage from past experiences which are an impediment weight. The baggage of slavery still exists on both sides. We hear people say why do I have to pay for the sins of my fore-fathers, which presupposes that it is only the forefathers who sinned. That is not the case. It continues. Everyone will pay for their own sins, no matter what words you utter, so bear in mind that God makes the decision regarding who will pay. By the hand of God, blacks are no longer slaves in America. He used people and circumstances to accomplish it. You can liken it to God delivering Israel under the hands of Pharoah in the Bible. We all have unconscious biases. That is why we have to renew our minds with God's Word. Unquestionably, blacks and other minority groups have been victimized in ways well beyond what I write here. Though victims, we do not have to have a victim's mentality. If we take a victim's mentality, evil wins. We can choose our attitudes, honor God, and grow spiritually.

Though unaware, nonminorities are also victims through self-doing. We are already born with a sinful nature. When some teach the superiority of one race over another, they teach sin. For those who teach you or have taught you against another race, they did not do you a favor. Teaching racism sows seeds that reap evil. This is not all there is, "For we must all appear before the judgment seat of Christ, so that each of us may receive what is due us for the things done while in the body, whether good or bad" (2 Corinthians 5:10).

Seminars and conversations can be helpful, but they can never solve the problem. We have talked about it for hundreds of years. Many close their ears to hearing about racial issues. Closed ears come from closed hearts. Only God can change closed, cold hearts to open, warm hearts of love. For we must all appear before the judgment seat of Christ, so that each of us may receive what is due us for the things done while in the body, whether good or bad. You cannot mock God. Payday will surely come regarding racism. You wonder whether the racial unrest is part of the reaping for racism. "Do not be deceived: God cannot be mocked. A man reaps what he sows" (Galatians 6:7).

We can align our thoughts and action with what God says about the matter by renewing our minds from sinful thinking that does not align with what God says (Romans 12:2, Ephesians 4:23). Change comes from within. Cultural behavior against some groups is so wrong that the legislature enacted laws against discrimination, namely laws against racial, gender, age, religious, and other discrimination. If we apply biblical principles, the only law we need is the law of God. Consequences exist for violating human law. Those consequences are less than the consequences for breaking God's law.

I used to think that everyone was aware of the country's racial issues. I was astonished when a well-educated, intelligent white Christian woman said to me in 2010 that she had no knowledge before then that the country had a race problem. Before I heard her say that I would say things like, "we know it, they know it, and the whole world knows it," but she didn't. In preparation for a racial reconciliation forum in 2020, two white men on the panel told me that many white people still don't believe we have a racial problem or understand it. Again, we don't all share the same experiences.

Embracing racial differences and working together can help us become more like Christ, and work toward unity. Politicians often talk about the national debt and not wanting to leave debt to our children. I fully agree. We also should not want to leave the racial divide to the next generation. "If a house is divided against itself, that house cannot stand" (Mark 3:25). Nor can a nation. Imploding from within because of sin may be a more significant threat than an outside enemy.

I would be remiss to talk about race without mentioning Dr. Tony Evans's book *Oneness Embraced*. It gave me greater insight and understanding of the issue from a biblical perspective. The book is a comprehensive treatise on the racial divide that shines the light of Scripture on the matter for vision clarity. Evans states that God has postponed His involvement in the racial divide because His church has not appropriately responded to the issue.

> The truth that has been missed is that God does much of what He does predicated on what His church is or is not doing (Ephesians 3:10). In the same way that God's purpose, presence, and power in the Old Testament was to flow from His people and through the temple into the world (Ezekiel 47:1–12), even so today it should flow from

the church into the broader society. When the church fails to act in concert with God's prescribed agenda, then God often chooses to postpone His active involvement until His people are prepared to respond. [10]

We hinder God's active involvement related to the race issue and all issues of our lives when we do not live by biblical principles. My sister Ruth Barnett says it well, "If God is not in it, you need to be out of it." To close this chapter, I go back to the last two lines in the poem "Differences." "The chief aim of life should be to bring Him glory. When it's all said and done, what will be your story?"

CHAPTER 10

GENERATIONAL DIFFERENCES

G od is the King. We are His subjects. When God designed His world of people, He gave rules for an orderly society. He comprised His world of diverse age groups who live in generational cycles, from one generation to the next. The psalmist understood the importance of generations, "One generation commends your works to another; they tell of your mighty acts" (Psalm 145:4).

GENERATIONAL RESPONSIBILITY

God structured age groups to interrelate for our spiritual growth and social well-being. The basic generational difference is seen in the family structure. Parents and children are different generations. Scripture instructs both parents and children how to interrelate. Scripture directs parents to train children in righteous ways (see Proverbs 22:26). It also directs parents to not exasperate children to anger (see Ephesians 6:4). Scripture instructs children to obey their parents as it is the right thing to do (see Ephesians 6:1). When we see the family operate biblically, we see healthy families of more unity and harmony between different generations.

Continuing with differences and social order, Scripture instructs husbands and wives to submit to each other mutually. It also designates the husband as the head of the wife (see Ephesians 5:21; 5:23). We do not see as many leadership fights at work, school, or church, as in the family, though we see conflict everywhere. Perhaps we see it more prevalently in the home because of the misunderstanding or misapplication of the husband's leadership role. Nonetheless, it is God's world; God's rules.

Scripture tells us the husband should love his wife as he loves himself and give his life for her, as Christ gave His life for His bride, the church. As the head, the husband is supposed to see after the wife's and family's well-being (see Ephesians 5:25-30). When we see family life authentically practiced according to biblical principles, we see fewer fights. A wife's submission to her husband is submission to God (see Ephesians 5:22). People talk about a wife's submission, but we hear less about the mutual submission of the husband and wife as stated in Ephesians 5:21. When we apply biblical principles, family members grow spiritually and unify for oneness mandated by Scripture.

Scripture does not leave out the community to aid in generational social well-being. "It takes a village" is a prevalent principle throughout the relationship building process. Scripture specifically instructs older men to mentor younger men and the older women to mentor the younger women (see Titus 2:4; 2:6). It gives instruction to teach the younger generation of men and women to live self-controlled lives of integrity (see Titus 2:4-7). The qualification to teach the younger generation is not just age, but requires older men and women to model what they teach by living reverent lives, worthy of respect (see Titus 2:4-7).

When we look at how intergenerational relationships are supposed to operate overall, we will see parents watch out for the children's welfare by training them. Parents also encourage and build up children. Children cooperate with parents in being trained. Spouses respect each other and live in peace and harmony together. Additionally, the Christian community of older men and older women helps across generational lines to teach the young men and women who receive instructions from the older generation. Unfortunately, that is not what we see today.

The earth continually rotates on its axis. The sun timely rises and sets daily, and the ever-existing moon shows itself at night. God structured order for His physical universe and structured order for His created humanity. The problem comes when we don't line up with biblical principles. God has designed us to need one another generationally. He designed us for peace and unity. Embrace the differences and enjoy the journey as you learn, grow, and know across generational lines.

God gave generational cycles from life to death. We consider generations to be those born within a certain period. Researchers do cultural studies of generational groups and identify a group's beliefs and values. Throughout the book, I will reference research and scientific studies findings. All truth is God's truth. The research indicates commonalities within the groups, which are guidelines, not necessarily stereotypes. Generally, the differences are what motivates the group, how they communicate, and how they do things. Researchers categorize six generations.

GENERATIONAL CATEGORIES (BY BIRTH YEARS)

1. *Greatest Generation: 1901 – 1927.* They are a hard-working group who follow the hierarchal chain of command. They like acknowledgment and rewards for hard work but are not technologically astute. Impacting world events include the Depression, World War II. FDR Administration.

2. *Silent Generation: 1928 – 1945.* Some believe their perceived silence was due to the belief that it was best to say nothing due to the McCarthy era making unfounded accusations of communism and treason. Impacting life issues include World War II, the Depression, and the Korean War.

3. *Boomers (aka Me First generation): 1946 -1964.* Boomers prefer a consensual leadership style. They like to be acknowledged through raises and promotions and define themselves by their career status. They challenge the rules and are adept

at technology. Impacting world events include the Civil Rights Movement, The Cold War, Vietnam War, and the Nixon/Watergate scandal.

4. *Generation X (aka Who Cares generation): 1965 – 1980.* They do not trust leadership and prefer a collaborative leadership style. They love fun and are self-reliant. They work hard and play hard. Generation X will refuse a promotion if their home life suffers. They are technologically involved. Impacting world events include the Challenger disaster, the Aids epidemic, Berlin Wall, diversity, and the Ronald Reagan/George Bush administrations.

5. *Millennial Generation: 1981 – 1996.* They question authority, prefer self-leadership, and believe learning is a two-way street. Further, they are motivated by independence, flexibility, and opportunity. They live technologically with cell phones, texting, instant messaging, and the like. Impacting world events include the internet, school violence, and the Iraq War.

6. *Generation Z (aka Post Millennials): 1997 -* Though technologically astute like the Millennials, Gen Z has distinct differences. Millennials like to enjoy their job. Gen Z sees a job strictly for the money. They are entrepreneurial and prefer face-to-face communication, whether via FaceTime, Skype, or otherwise. They are inclusive related to diversity and like to be heard. Most will not be able to remember a time when cell phones and social media did not exist. Impacting world events are still evolving for this period and include the September 11, 2001 World Trade Center attack, Barack Obama/Donald Trump administrations, racial unrest/George Floyd killing, COVID-19, and the January 6, 2021 Capitol insurrection.

A Boomer mom, Ellen, and her Millennial daughter, Alice, argue based on a lack of understanding of differences. Ellen gets frustrated and does not understand why Alice questions authority at work. Alice believes her boss can learn from her as well as she can learn from the boss. Alice is independent and lives technologically through constant text messaging and social media. The mother-daughter duo improved their relationship when they learned to respect their differences. Each grew from allowing and respecting the differences.

A few years ago, I noted that some of my church's older members did not like the new and younger choir director's louder music contrasted to his predecessor. The older congregants preferred hymns and soft flowing music. One Sunday, during a fast rhythmic, booming song, an elderly woman frowned, stuck her fingers in her ears, shook her head in a negative gesture, and said, "too loud." Some saw humor in her behavior, some saw disrespect, and others showed no reaction. The pastor had instructed the choir director to include diverse music genres for the generationally diverse congregation to enjoy. By rejecting differences in the music preference of the younger generation, the elderly woman failed to allow for differences and probably learned nothing from the experiences and somewhat disrupted peace during church service. We can advance spiritually, curtail conflict, and have more peaceful relationships when we recognize and allow for the differences of others.

For about 20 years, the Boomers were the largest generation. In 1991, the Millennials passed the Boomers' number when the Millennials reached over 72 million. Marketers key in on Millennials because of its growing population, though Boomers still maintain a high number. Eventually, one by one, all the current generations pass off the scene like forgone generations, while others arrive to take their place. Since we must interact with varying age groups while on this earth, it would be expedient to allow for differences for spiritual growth and unity. God desires holiness and peace for us.

The congregants in the Bible found fault with the disciple Timothy and complained about his youth. Paul instructed Timothy to let no one have disdain for him because of his young age (1 Timothy 4:12). God calls people of various age groups. Paul encouraged Timothy to live as an example despite the complaints about his young age because modeling it, teaching, and preaching would compensate for his age.

We continue to hear complaints about and from various age groups and see intolerance of other age groups. None of these problems would exist, whether it be generational, race, or anything else, if we submitted to godly principles and cooperated with the Holy Spirit that God gave to convict us of sin. He never leads us astray. Yet, we often do not use the empowerment God gave us and choose to sin instead. God designed His world for a cycle of generationally diverse age groups.

Just like seasons of the year come and go, generations come and go off the scene. Millions of people have inhabited the earth and gone off the scene since God's creation. In a few years, all of our current generations will be gone, and new ones will exist, but God's throne is forever (see Hebrews 1:8).

GENERATIONS PASS AWAY

Scripture is sobering and profound regarding generations and our fleeting lives. In this section and the next section, I let Scripture speak for itself. Ponder the matter regarding generations as you read.

"Joseph died, and all his brothers and all that generation" (Exodus 1:6).

"For David, after he had served the purpose of God in his own generation, fell asleep, and was laid among his fathers and underwent decay" (Acts 13:36).

"After that whole generation had been gathered to their ancestors, another generation grew up who knew neither the Lord nor what he had done for Israel" (Judges 2:10).

"They would not be like their ancestors—a stubborn and rebellious generation whose hearts were not loyal to God, whose spirits were not faithful to him" (Psalm 78:8).

"For the wise, like the fool, will not be long remembered; the days have already come when both have been forgotten. Like the fool, the wise too must die" (Ecclesiastes 2:16).

We will serve our time and the next generations will come.

GOD'S THRONE NEVER PASSES AWAY

While generations pass off the scene, God is constant and reigns forever (see Isaiah 9:7). Reflect and think about the below scriptural passages.

"Now to him who is able to do immeasurably more than all we ask or imagine, according to his power that is at work within us, to him be glory in the church and in Christ Jesus throughout all generations, for ever and ever! Amen" (Ephesians 3:20-21).

"You, LORD, reign forever; your throne endures from generation to generation" (Lamentations 5:19).

"Your kingdom is an everlasting kingdom, and your dominion endures through all generations. The LORD is trustworthy in all he promises and faithful in all he does" (Psalm 145:13).

Our intergenerational battles are futile. It will all pass away. While on this side of eternity, we can enjoy what God gave us intergenerationally. We are already made in His image. He called us to a ministry of reconciliation for peace and unity, not a ministry of reconstructing people to our way of thinking or doing things. Pursue unity and peace within differences and benefit therefrom.

CHAPTER 11

GENDER

An old nursery rhyme says little girls are made of sugar and spice and everything nice, whereas little boys are made of snips and snails and puppy dog tails. We know that is not true, but it points out gender differences more than the physical. Men and women have battled since the fall with Adam and Eve in the Garden of Eden.

God created men and women differently. Science caught up with God's creation and discovered that God wired men's and women's brains differently. God regards genders the same when it comes to spiritual matters and gave men and women the same spiritual gifts. Men and women are all His children according to Scripture. "There is neither Jew nor Gentile, neither slave nor free, nor is there male and female, for you are all one in Christ Jesus" (Galatians 3:28).

The Bible uses different terms to describe gender. The Hebrew word for "male" is *zākār* and "female" is *nêqēbâ*. The Hebrew reference is to male and female rather than man and woman. Diversity of gender is part of God's creative purpose to reproduce and replenish the earth. The physical appearances of males and females differ, and we use feminine and masculine to describe the difference. Despite physical differences, Scripture is clear that God made both in His image (See Genesis 1:27). Being made in His image means He gave us will, intellect, and emotions. Each is equally intelligent and equal in endowment with spiritual gifts.

As relates to the differences, God made males and females to complement each other. In Genesis 2:18, God proclaimed that it was not good for Adam (man) to be alone, so He created Eve (woman) to be suited to help Adam. In our theme of unity and oneness note that Genesis explicitly stated that Adam and Eve were to become "one." "That is why a man leaves his father and mother and is united to his wife, and they become one flesh" (Genesis 2:24). Again, though different, designed for oneness. "God created humanity as male and female. Although gender differences are evident in behaviour and role, Scripture teaches the equality and complementarity of the sexes."[11]

This chapter is not about the biblically prescribed roles of men and women in marriage but about how God wants gender unity and oneness within gender diversity. In the larger context of all believers, God instructs unity and oneness in the body of Christ across all diverse lines. In the smaller context of marriage (husband and wife), God says the two shall become one. Note the word "become." Scripture refers to oneness in sexual intimacy and becoming one in a peaceful marital relationship. As mentioned previously, Gary Thomas asserts in *Sacred Marriage*, God made marriage to make us holy more than to make us happy.[12] Within marriage they unify as they grow through adverse experiences. God's aim is to make us holy—Christlike spiritual advancement.

When God declared that it is "not good for man to be alone," He was saying there is something more that man needs for the ideal situation. Thus, He created someone different than Adam needed beyond himself. The diverse gender form of Eve was created to benefit Adam.

Harvard conducted an MRI imaging study of emotion in children's brains with interesting findings. Children process emotion in the amygdala, which is far from the cerebral cortex of the brain. Brain activity for girls moves from the amygdala to the cerebral area of the brain as girls mature. The study revealed that this does not happen at the same level as boys grow, making it harder for males to tell how they feel. It is generally the opposite for women.[13] Recognition of these differences could curtail conflict as each allows for the differences of others.

APPRECIATING GENDER DIFFERENCES

Practicing patience and love with differences helps us grow. There are things in women's DNA that can wear men out if they do not accept differences. Men generally will not communicate at the level as most women. Lest I overgeneralize, some men speak excessively, and some women do not. Typically, women are wired differently for communication and emotions, as scientific studies prove. The Bible speaks of a quarrelsome wife. "Better to live on a corner of the roof than share a house with a quarrelsome wife" (Proverbs 25:24). Some people use that scriptural passage to laugh at and ridicule women. I use it here as more of an educational tool. It directs men and women: (1) directs women to not be contentious because it causes conflict, and (2) tells men that if the woman is contentious, you have been warned; it is better to get out of the way than enter the conflict. That may not be a strict theological interpretation, but if a fire is coming at you, move out of the way!

Studies also show that little boys are exhilarated by the possibility of danger, whereas little girls are fearful. That shares insight on why my brothers loved playing tricks to scare their sisters. Boys fight twenty times more than girls and usually end up better friends after a fight, unlike little girls who seldom fight, but when they do, the feelings last longer.[14] Boys are more likely to overestimate their abilities, whereas girls are more likely to underestimate their abilities.[15] Failure to recognize and bear with differences in men's and women's behavior can be the source of conflict, particularly if you devalue one group.

One lady tells of a story where she was distraught concerning her divorce while her brother was at her home visiting her. He looked greatly concerned, balled up his fist, and said, "I don't know how to say this other than, you need to man-up." Urbandictionary.com defines man-up as "to act following established masculine roles in a given situation, implying courage and responsibility"—not the tears she displayed. Her brother's concerned look while balling up his fist to make a strength gesture caused her to laugh amid her pain. Her brother showed care for her. He valued her at a time when she needed support. His attitude made a difference, even though his frame of reference, "man-up," was not the same frame of reference for a woman. Though the brother's reference frame was different, she allowed for the difference because of his love and care. Love made the difference. Bear with one another in love (see Ephesians 4:2).

The book titled *Leadership and the Sexes* provides information that is helpful to show how gender science can be used to create business success:[16] All truth is God's truth.

1. Neither brain is superior, but the blood flow in a female's brain is 15-20 percent higher than in a male's brain, which causes different parts of a female's brain to work simultaneously, unlike a male's brain. Multitasking comes more easily for women than men.

2. The male's brain rests many more times than a female's brain daily, explaining why they listen differently, complete tasks differently, become bored, and hold a basic conversation differently. The fact that their brain naturally rests more than a woman's brain may account for sayings, like "a woman's work is never done."

3. Each is equally intelligent, but because of how their brains process differently, they focus on different things, results, ideas, and products.

4. A male's hippocampus, his major memory center, is less active than a woman's. A man may be less likely to express emotion because there is less linkage between the memory center and the brain's word center.

5. A female's more active occipital and parietal lobes can affect conflict communication and negotiations. Both males and females can negotiate well but get to the result in different ways.

6. Because the male temporal lobe is generally less active than the female, women can better transfer the information they read and hear into written form than males. Because they

use words differently at times, the combination of both can maximize business success.

The gender differences are complementary but can naturally lead to conflict when sinful intolerance of differences produces friction, resulting in conflict fire. We can use gender differences conflict to help us grow in Christlike character. In *Sacred Marriage*, Thomas asserts that the issues in marriage provide opportunities to practice Christlikeness to produce holiness. It is interesting that as I was writing this section, I received a phone call from a friend who asked me to pray for her marriage. She was concerned about her husband's lack of communication and openness at the level she desired. Unless something else was going on, it is just the way he is wired. Otherwise, she and her husband have a great relationship. He treats her well. She does not desire to work outside the home, and her husband emotionally and financially supports her decision. He does not physically or verbally abuse her. However, he does not communicate with her at the level she prefers. Earth is not heaven. Adapting to differences helps us have more peace of mind.

Our progressive spiritual growth is sometimes painful, as are growing pains in the natural from infancy to adulthood. Each stage has issues to grapple with and grow through from infancy, early childhood, adolescence, young adult, middle age, and the elderly. Deciding to be content in circumstances could be helpful. When we submit all these issues to God and value each other, we grow. When we grow, we better conform to God's law of unity.

We can also have conflict within the same gender due to personalities and other differences. Women's temperaments are such that women whack each other in ways that men do not. In *Leading Women Who Wound*, Dr. Sue Edwards teaches women how to deal with other women who are insensitive, manipulative, or plain mean.[17] The male ego is said to be fragile as it reflects man's need for approval, validation, and a sense of worth and value.[18] The "ego" wiring of men can lead to conflict with women and other men. Clashes within the same gender can also be used to grow us as we learn to bear with one another.

PART 4

GOD USES CHANGEABLE DIFFERENCES TO GROW US

The previous section covered differences associated with the diversity theory that God created human diversity to give us naturally arising opportunities to practice biblical principles to produce Christlike character growth. This section continues the theme that diversity encounters can lead to holiness, but whereas the previous section dealt with unchangeable differences, this section starts the discussion of changeable differences.

CHAPTER 12

RELIGION

A common statement says, "never talk about religion or politics," because both subjects lead to conflict. Even Linus in the "Peanuts" comic strip said, "There are three things I have learned never to discuss with people…religion, politics, and the Great Pumpkin." Contrary to popular belief, I talk about both religion and politics in this book for the reason popular belief says to avoid it—it leads to conflict. This book is a conflict resolution book. I address it to shed scriptural light on religion and politics to curtail conflict. Avoid letting popular beliefs have a chilling effect on addressing issues as appropriate.

With this chapter, we have moved from God *created* unchangeable differences to make us holy to God *uses* changeable differences to make us holy. Whether unchangeable or changeable differences, God can use them to make us holy. Both can work together for our good to conform us into Christlike holiness. "And we know that in all things God works for the good of those who love him, who have been called according to his purpose" (Romans 8:28). It is God doing the work, orchestrating matters behind the scenes to work benefit in us through spiritual growth. We know differences have the potential to cause friction rub to lead to conflict unless we practice biblical principles during the encounter. God created us free-will beings who may choose to change differences like religion or political party.

A Pew Research Center article dated 2-1-2021, titled "One-in-five Americans Who Have Been Harassed Say It Was Because of Their Religion" illustrates conflict associated with religion. The research participants said they had been abused for their religion in at least one of the following behaviors: physical threats, stalking, sustained harassment, sexual harassment, offensive name-calling, or purposeful embarrassment. Historically religious persecution was such an issue that it became part of the First Amendment of the United States Constitution, which guarantees freedom of religion, among other liberties. Yet, many people continue to attack those of differing faiths. Religious conflict gives us assignments as ministers of reconciliation to bring peace out of conflict. The First Amendment nor any other legislation can do what only God can do to give a heart of love.

CHRISTIANITY DISTINGUISHED

Grace distinguishes Christianity from other faiths. No other religion gives grace to wrongdoers. Grace bestows a benefit we do not deserve and cannot earn. In other religions, you must do something in return for their god's favor. In Christianity, God loves imperfect people unconditionally. He died for us when we did nothing to deserve it and can never do anything to deserve it. But God demonstrates his own love for us in this: "While we were still sinners, Christ died for us" (Romans 5:8). Following is a summary of the Christian faith in the Apostles' Creed below.

The Apostles' Creed

I believe in God the Father Almighty, Maker of heaven and earth. And in Jesus Christ, His only Son, our Lord; Who was conceived by the Holy Spirit; born of the Virgin Mary; Suffered under Pontius Pilate; Was crucified, dead and buried; He descended into Hell; The third day He rose again from the dead; He ascended into heaven; And sitteth on the right hand of God the Father Almighty; From thence He shall come to judge the living and the dead. I believe in the Holy Spirit; The Holy Christian Church, the Communion of Saints; The Forgiveness of sins; The Resurrection of the body; And the life everlasting. Amen.

God made known Christ's mission in the Old Testament through prophecies. In the New Testament, Christ came to fulfill the promised Messiah spoken of in the Old Testament.

Jesus demonstrates that He is the fulfillment of the Old Testament prophecies throughout His ministry. Here are some examples of such instances: After Jesus read from Isaiah 61 in the synagogue, He closed the scrolls and said, "Today this Scripture is fulfilled in your hearing" (Luke 4:21). Another instance, in Luke chapter 24, Jesus joined some discouraged disciples after the resurrection. To deal with their discouragement, Jesus explains the Old Testament prophecies and how He is the fulfillment of them. The disciples said their hearts burned within as Jesus opened up the Scriptures to them (see Luke 4:32). The disciples preached the message that Jesus was the promised Messiah (see Acts 2:36-39; 3:18; 1 Corinthians 15:1-7). When a person accepts that Jesus is the promised Messiah who came to bring salvation to the world, that person is said to be "in the faith."

All Christians were at one time outside the faith, so be reminded of your spiritual beginnings. The apostle Paul describes himself as a former blasphemer, persecutor, and insolent opponent of God. He said he did it out of ignorance, but God's grace overflowed in him (see 1 Timothy 1:121-17). Like Paul, we were all sinners before coming to faith through grace. Like we changed, so can others.

Differences can bring conflict fires to practice love and allow for differences, which can help you grow. It can also be a witness of who Christ is in you that may lead others to accept Him. Those who reject Christ will be condemned. "There is a judge for the one who rejects me and does not accept my words; the very words I have spoken will condemn them at the last day" (John 12:48).

Some Jews expected Jesus to come in pomp, so they rejected Him and stirred up strife regarding Him. "But the Jews who refused to believe stirred up the other Gentiles and poisoned their minds against the brothers" (Acts 14:2). That is much like various religions stir up the minds of people against Christians today. They should not do such, nor should Christians be antagonistic toward other groups. Those who use hateful rhetoric about other religions will not aid in leading anyone to Christ. On the contrary, they will harm Christ's reputation. We are God's representatives on earth who can witness best by our behavior of love and peace. Jesus said whoever welcomes the foreigner, the naked and hungry welcomes him (see Matthew 25:35).

CONDEMNATION OF HATE

The most significant thing we can do is to show love as directed in the two greatest commandments to love God with everything in us and others as ourselves (See Matthew 22:36-40). That commandment includes loving people of other religions, even enemies.

> You have heard that it was said, "Love your neighbor and hate your enemy." But I tell you, love your enemies and pray for those who persecute you, that you may be children of your Father in heaven. He causes his sun to rise on the evil and the good, and sends rain on the righteous and the unrighteous (Matthew 5:43-45).

Never spew hate regarding others. Hatred is the strong emotion of detesting or despising someone. When we hate, we become guilty of the crime of murder. "Anyone who hates a brother or sister is a murderer, and you know that no murderer has eternal life residing in him" (1 John 3:15). Look at all the homicides in the country. It is because of hatred. When we hate, it ushers in the spirit of murder to be used by the devil for evil.

Distinguish worldly hatred and godly hatred. *Godly hatred* is righteous indignation or righteous anger toward that which is unholy. David recognized and accepted God's righteous anger toward him. "Against you, you only, have I sinned and done what is evil in your sight; so you are right in your verdict and justified when you judge" (Psalm 51:4).

Worldly hatred is unjustified and unrighteous anger that produces sinful, evil conduct because of hate toward someone or something. The culture recognizes the wrong of hate by enacting hate crime laws that carry penalties for hate crimes. Hate crimes are motivated by bias. An example of hatred leading to murder is the murders of three civil rights workers, two whites and one black (Michael Schwerner, Andrew Goodman, and James Chaney), referred to as the Mississippi Burning. They were ages 20, 21, and 24. Their young lives ended by the hate from the Ku Klux Klan because of their civil rights activism. It remains a puzzle that the Klan who profess Christianity burn the cross during hate conduct when the cross symbolizes Christ's love for all.

God condemns hate. "You have heard that it was said, 'Love your neighbor and hate your enemy.' But I tell you, love your enemies and pray for those who persecute you, that you may be children of your Father in heaven" (Matthew 5:43-45). God operates in realms beyond our capacity to grasp fully, as stated in Scripture, "Since ancient times no one has heard, no ear has perceived, no eye has seen any God besides you, who acts on behalf of those who wait for him" (Isaiah 64:4). Murder is a crime of hate. A LiveScience article titled "Murder May Spread Like Infectious Disease" states that scientific studies show murder is contagious with the capacity to spread like the flu. Of particular note, the article states, "What causes crime is one of the most studied, yet most elusive questions." The elusiveness of the reason is that they are looking at science when the cause is a spiritual matter related to human depravity. If those who hate understood the principle of love, respecting and bearing with one another, they and society could be helped.

HUMAN DEPRAVITY

Human "depravity" is a malady of all people brought about by the Fall in the Garden of Eden. It is the reason all humans have a corrupt nature. It explains our plight today in all spheres of life. Though we can do good deeds and have a conscience, our conscience is not reliable because our nature has been affected by the fall of man described in Genesis 3. Because of human depravity, murders and all manner of evil result. We see human depravity in small children's behavior, and we wonder why one so young could behave in such a way. It is in our nature. No one needs to teach a child to be selfish. James 4:1-3 tells us our fights and quarrels come from within us, our nature. Of course, those in Christ have a new nature and the power of the Holy Spirit to overcome.

CHRIST COMMENDS RIGHTEOUSNESS, REBUKES SIN

Authentic Christianity recognizes Christians don't always get it right. The book of Revelation refers to seven early churches. Of the seven churches, only two did not receive a rebuke from Christ. Four of the seven received commendations for righteous behavior and also a rebuke for unrighteous behavior. Only one of the seven churches received no commendation, only a rebuke, because it was a dead church. In each case of rebuke, Christ directed that they repent. Christ rebuked them for things like being lukewarm spiritually, adultery, compromise of the gospel, and tolerance of sin.

JESUS INTERACTED WITH DIVERSE GROUPS

Jesus is our example of how to interact with differences. Jesus came to save sinners, so He associated with various religious groups and sinners for which the Pharisees criticized Him (see Luke 7:34). Pharisees place people in bondage with lots of rules, but Christ came to set us free and give us life more abundantly (See Luke 14:18; John 10:10). By comparison, the Jews would have nothing to do with Samaritans (See John 4). Jesus did not follow the prejudices of the Jews against Samaritans or condemn sinners but loved them. He came to the earth to serve others, not to be served by others. (See Matthew 20:28). He expressed that the greatest people are those who serve others, not the self-focus of wanting others to serve you (See Matthew 20:25-28).

Jesus interacted both with the Samaritan woman at the well and the woman who was caught in adultery. The judgmental crowd wanted to stone the woman caught in adultery, but after Jesus dealt with the crowd, they left. He then told the woman that He did not condemn her, to go and discontinue sinning (See John 8:1-11). Likewise, we should not condemn others who differ from us. Distinguish the words "interact" and "fellowship." Jesus interacted with them. Christian fellowship is based on a vertical relationship with God of those involved. "Have nothing to do with the fruitless deeds of darkness, but rather expose them" (Ephesians 5:11). We are also instructed not to be deceived about bad company because it will corrupt our good character (see 1 Corinthians 15:33).

Jesus has a heart of compassion for people and went through all the towns sharing the good news and healing all their illnesses (See Matthew 9:35-36). He saw a harvest that needed laborers but found few laborers for the work (See Matthew 9:37). That is an indictment against those religious leaders of the day who did not meet the need of people. The people needed leadership, but few existed to lead them. We still need laborers today.

Whether we directly encounter those of other religions or discuss other religions with people of our faith, avoid condemnation as Christ did not condemn. He called us to be witnesses, not critics. Treat everyone with respect and dignity. Lack of practicing biblical principles regarding differences leads to conflict. So how can such encounters bring peace? Applying biblical responses helps us grow and shine light to show the way in our dark world.

> You are the light of the world. A town built on a hill cannot be hidden. Neither do people light a lamp and put it under a bowl. Instead, they put it on its stand, and it gives light to everyone in the house. In the same way, let your light shine before others, that they may see your good deeds and glorify your Father in heaven (Matthew 5:14-16).

A CHRISTIAN NATION

America has had a reputation of being a Christian nation, which we have watched steadily erode to the degree that many no longer see us as a Christian nation. However, as Jesus did for the seven churches in

Revelation, commend the good, but do not ignore the bad. Rebuke it. The enactment of the National Day of Prayer in 1952 is a good thing. It calls for people to turn to God for prayer. Each year the President signs a proclamation calling for Americans to pray. Federal statute requires the proclamation.

> The President shall issue each year a proclamation designating the first Thursday in May as a National Day of Prayer on which the people of the United States may turn to God in prayer and meditation at churches, in groups, and as individuals (36 U.S.C. § 119).

We can never have enough prayer for our nation. "Pray continually" (1 Thessalonians 5:17). Yet, applying biblical principles to live the Christian life is different from mouthing words of prayer. Our actions reflect what is in our hearts. If our actions don't match our prayers, we stand indicted. Solomon, the wisest man who ever lived, wrote the books of Ecclesiastes, Proverbs, and Song of Solomon. He concluded that everything is meaningless outside of God, who has placed eternity in our hearts (see Ecclesiastes 3: 11). We have all heard there is a hole in man's heart, meaning something is missing. It is God. Solomon concluded that the aim of life is for us to do good by keeping God's commandments. "Now all has been heard; here is the conclusion of the matter: Fear God and keep his commandments, for this is the duty of all mankind. For God will bring every deed into judgment, including every hidden thing, whether it is good or evil" (Ecclesiastes 12:13-14) That is what is missing in lives, keeping God's commandments.

People do not naturally employ peacemaking practices in the midst of differences conflicts. Conflict resolution requires a Kingdom perspective. When faced with conflict, we often drop the "glorify God" ball and advance our position disregarding God and others. First Corinthians 10:31 mandates that we glorify God in whatever we do. It did not say except for religious conflict. God exempts no one from the mandate to glorify God. To glorify God means to advertise God and make Him look good. Behavior that glorifies God stands against wrong and fosters peace.

SITTING FROGS OR NOT?

Romans 12:2 tells us to renew our minds to God-honoring thinking. Such thinking will bring God-honoring behavior. It appears we let the culture transform Christians more than Christians changing the culture. We stay silent as the culture adopts ungodly agendas. We are like the sitting frog fable. If you put a frog in hot water, it will immediately jump out. However, if you put it in water that is heated gradually, the frog will sit comfortably, not noticing the steadily warming water until it's too late—the frog is cooked. We have ignored and stayed silent about evil so long that we can be likened to sitting frogs that get cooked. Evil prances about while we have allowed a chilling effect to be put on speaking up for fear of backlash on many issues. We need not be sitting frogs. Through Christ, we are the only hope for the world. "If my people, who are called by my name, will humble themselves and pray and seek my face and turn from their wicked ways, then I will hear from heaven, and I will forgive their sin and will heal their land" (2 Chronicles 7:14). We know the land needs healing. "Pray continually" (1 Thessalonians 5:17). The National Day of Prayer is in accord with 2 Chronicles 7:14, but the passage has several facets beyond prayer: (1) seek God's face; (2) turn from our wicked ways, and then God will heal our land.

CHAPTER 13

POLITICS

Like race and religion, the topic of politics is too extensive to cover in one chapter, so we cover it broadly here. Politics, the activities that surround the governance of society, is diverse and complex. It leads to battles within local, state, and national governments and between nations. Individuals also war about political parties, political positions, and their preferred politicians.

We see vile behavior associated with the polarization of political parties. The motive of a thing determines the morality of a thing. However, we don't always know the underlying motives connected to the conduct of politicians. The dictionary contains many definitions for politics. We use a portion of Merriam Webster's description:

> The art or science concerned with winning and holding control over a government; political affairs or business, especially the competition between competing interest groups or individuals for power and leadership; and political activities characterized by artful and often dishonest practices.

From the definition, we key in on certain words: holding control; competition for power; characterized by dishonest statements. We continuously see these aspects of the definition in competitive fights to control an outcome. We also witness it in dishonest practices for power and control. The absence of a moral compass brings heightened division and strife. There is no wonder that evil prevails where we have selfish ambition and unhealthy competition between parties. "For where you have envy and selfish ambition, there you find disorder and every evil practice" (James 3:16). Whatever the motivation behind the evil practices we see, we know God is not the generator of it (See 1 Corinthians 14:33).

When we see politicians pursue power and control by evil means, we hear, "that's just politics." Well, that's just awful. Dishonesty and hateful vitriol are on full display. The division will not fare well for the country. "If a house is divided against itself, that house cannot stand" (Mark 3:25). We cannot stand divided and watch our ongoing decline. Many have become desensitized to our plight and accept dishonesty and poor behavior—"that's just politics." Yet, if we learn to practice what is good and right, respect each other, and allow differences of opinions, we can improve and unify more as a nation. "Righteousness exalts a nation, but sin condemns any people" (Proverbs 14:34).

I can think of no other arena outside of politics where venom could continue without consequences. We would not accept such bad behavior from family relations, employees, friends, or church leaders. Politicians' poor behavior extends to constituents who join and spew hate. Many cheer bad behavior from political favorites. May I have the envelope please? And the winner for the loudest, rudest, most combative person is Politician X—and constituents applaud.

Though free speech is also for governmental officials to discuss issues freely, you would think an official's intent to deceive the public would be an exception. You would think that politicians have a fiduciary duty that includes truth, honor, and statesmanship. Political battles exist worldwide. I used to say we have not physically fought in our governmental chambers like other countries, but the Capitol Insurrection of January 6, 2021, stopped that statement.

Those of differing political viewpoints are vilified and viewed as enemies and unamerican. The doctrine of separation of church and state is designed to keep church and governmental affairs separate.

Without giving my opinion of the doctrine, I will say that some politicians claim to be Christians during an election cycle. However, we may not hear it again until the next election cycle when it suits them for votes. All politicians do not act righteously, neither do all lawyers, doctors, police officers, teachers, or any other profession. People go about sinning and disregarding sin. "Righteousness exalts a nation, but sin condemns any people" (Proverbs 14:34).

In his "Drum Major Instinct" sermon, Dr. Martin Luther King, Jr pointed out that humans are naturally inclined to want to be out front. Why not be out front with good behavior, omitting self-serving motives and actions. What is good for the country? Whether Christian or not, acceptable standards of civility exist though steadily being undermined. Everyone can try to put good out front. However, it is a mandate for Christians.

EYES ON POLITICIANS

We see the lousy behavior of Congress when a President gives the State of the Union address in the House chamber. We observe stoic faces toward the President if he is not of their party. We observe scowling at various statements the President makes. They cheer for their own and sneer at the other. It is disrespectful behavior in disregard of the office of the President regardless of the political party. They do it boldly and publicly also in disrespect of the viewing public, themselves, and the offices they hold. This type of behavior is not reserved for the State of the Union but is ongoing between parties. Better deportment from our elected officials would serve them well, their constituents, and the nation.

We need governmental authority. It comes from God (see Romans 13:1). And governmental authority is supposed to be for our good. "For the one in authority is God's servant for your good" (Romans 13:4). Imagine the anarchy that would exist without governmental rule, however Scripture assumes good rulership. "He that ruleth over men must be just, ruling in the fear of God" (2 Samuel 23:3 KJV). Scripture instructs people to submit to governing authorities, who are to provide justice for each person, promote the good, and punish evil (see Romans 13:1-7, 1 Peter 2:13-14). If governmental officials act righteously, we would see more unity despite differences.

EYES ON "WE THE PEOPLE"

In the Gettysburg address, Abraham Lincoln said we are a government "of the people, by the people and for the people." We expect politicians to solve problems when "we the people" are part of the problem. If the people are corrupt, they will elect corrupt officials. Some people never disagree with anything their preferred politician says. Because we favor a politician does not make everything he or she says right. Agree with what you can and disagree when appropriate. We become part of the problem if we do otherwise.

"We the people" are responsible for educating ourselves to understand the issues. During an election, I saw a news reporter interviewing people on the street. One lady said she would never vote for candidate X because she did not like him. When asked why she did not like him, she could only respond, "I just don't like him." What policies do you not like? She knew nothing of the issues or his position on any subject and looked embarrassed. Indeed, it is difficult for us to understand political positions because we primarily hear attacks on the other person and less about the issues. When you add deception, it becomes even more difficult to decipher through the rubbish. Political debates appear to be a "gotcha" game and news cycle ratings maneuver. That is why we must be diligent to seek truth.

I have wondered if laws should be enacted that make knowingly dishonest political practices illegal because it misleads the public. "We the people" are entitled to know about governmental affairs. Since we are entitled to know about the affairs of government, we are entitled to honesty about those matters.

Christians can be part of the problem. That is why God gives us the ability to confess sin. We need to hold ourselves accountable and government officials responsible. Some make the statement that God is more like my political party. The issue is not how God lines up with our political party but how our political party lines up with God. Some professed Christians and non-Christians mistreat each other. Unless a position is illegal or immoral, compromise for the good of the country on differences of perspectives. Compromise if it is an opinion or perspective, but never compromise God's standards. Stand on righteous standards. A government divided against itself won't stand. Without compromise, it's like playing tug of war with a rubber band. You get nowhere with both sides pulling in a different direction. The band breaks when it is stretched so taut that it pops apart. Another way to say it is how much progress do we make if I block your agenda for 4 years and you block my agenda for four years?

EYES ON BOTH POLITICIANS AND "WE THE PEOPLE"

By nature sheep are dumb. They scatter and can't find their way without the shepherd's protection. The Bible analogizes humans to dumb sheep. "We all, like sheep, have gone astray, each of us has turned to our own way; and the LORD has laid on him the iniquity of us all" (Isaiah 53:6). Dumb sheep citizens and dumb sheep politicians can share the blame. We have put our hope in politicians when the evidence is clear; they are not the answer. Jesus protects His sheep if we allow Him rather than going our stubborn way. Authentic Christians know God's voice and follow Him (John 10:27-28). We can compare Christ to a good shepherd who lays down his life for his sheep, and compare politicians to a hired hand. "I am the good shepherd. The good shepherd lays down his life for the sheep. The hired hand is not the shepherd and does not own the sheep. So when he sees the wolf coming, he abandons the sheep and runs away. Then the wolf attacks the flock and scatters it" (John 10:11-12). We need politicians, but I make the point they are not God. Because of differences, the country flips and flops from party to party during election cycles when we become unhappy with the majority party's leadership. For the most part, the cycle repeats itself, rotating from Democrats to Republicans in office.

EYES ON DEPRAVITY

Let's revisit human depravity spoken of in the chapter on religion. It refers to humanity's corrupt nature. Because of human depravity, we have political chaos, verbal and physical assault, family disruption, murders, serial killers, terrorists, genocide, wars between nations, and all manner of evil. Corruption flows from the individual to families, cities, states, countries, and worldwide corruption. That applies to politicians and all of life. Without God's Spirit in us, we remain helpless to control it.

It's hard to know the answer to some of the failures in our American experiment, called democracy. Nothing will ever be perfect. However, imperfection does not mean we cannot endeavor to improve instead of getting worse. Because politicians and citizens do not manage political differences, matters continue on a downhill trajectory. It is noteworthy that neither party contains all of "we the people." That is why we need to compromise. Yet, democracy is not the problem. Depraved people are the problem.

Like individuals can improve, so can the government. Constituents parrot their party or politicians without independent assessment or thought. No matter how right we believe our political party to be, none are flawless; no political party, no human. The only correct standard is God. To quote Martin Luther King, Jr again, "We must live together as brothers or perish together as fools." When we encounter political differences, we can respect each other as valuable creations of God. We can disagree with a position without trying to destroy the person with whom we disagree. We are all in the same boat, humanity's boat. Allowing for differences and compromising regarding viewpoints are critical needs. Compromising for peace is better than hostility that will lead to doom. God desires that we live in a peaceful, orderly society.

Pride is at the heart of failure to work together. To work together, you have to be considerate of and respect others. In a presidential leadership conference on C-Span, I saw former presidents of different parties (George W. Bush and Bill Clinton) come together for society's benefit, absent political division. They partnered their affiliated libraries and the libraries of George H.W. Bush and Lyndon B. Johnson to launch the Presidential Leadership Scholars program. They recognized they could accomplish more together than divided. Our differences can separate, divide, and foster conflict. It was encouraging to see them work together across political party lines. Harry S. Truman said, "It is amazing what you can accomplish if you do not care who gets the credit." The American public would prefer to hear what both parties accomplished together for the country's good. We often hear politicians state at the end of speeches, "May God bless the United States of America." God has requirements for blessings.

A ceasefire is a suspension of hostile activities. It cannot last because it is only proforma for a period and does not reach the heart. For those who cannot do it on an ongoing basis, perhaps an annual, semi-annual, or quarterly ceasefire day of hostilities in the political arena could help. It would require allowing for and respecting others' right to differ without treating them as enemies to be destroyed. The United Nations has an International Day of Peace. What about a periodic political ceasefire?

GOD'S RULES EXIST FOR OUR GOOD

God's rule is peace. Christians and non-Christians, politicians, and constituents spew hateful rhetoric toward one another and need prayer. Scripture tells us to pray for political leaders and all those in authority to live in an orderly society.

> I urge, then, first of all, that petitions, prayers, intercession and thanksgiving be made for all people—for kings and all those in authority, *that we may live peaceful and quiet lives in all godliness and holiness.* This is good, and pleases God our Savior, who wants all people to be saved and to come to a knowledge of the truth (1 Timothy 2:1-4 italics added for emphasis).

Evil drowns out Christian voices because of fear of speaking out, whereas we have allowed a chilling effect on standing up for righteousness, while others boldly strut about displaying sinful behavior. We have nothing to fear. "You, LORD, will keep the needy safe and will protect us forever from the wicked, who freely strut about when what is vile is honored by the human race" (Psalm 12:8).

For politicians who stand for right or vote their conscience, the hateful voices seem to come through louder. A congresswoman recently stood by her convictions and is currently paying the consequences because she dared to differ from her political party. Others have done the same. Those who stand for what they believe do not compromise their integrity and can feel good about themselves for not having been bought for power, prestige, or position. The apostle Peter made a statement when it came to standing for righteousness over culture: "We must obey God rather than human beings" (Acts 5:29).

Be careful when you go with the crowd into mob rule lawlessness. Civil activism is fine, but hate and violence are not acceptable. The First Amendment prescribes peaceful assembly. The operational word is "peaceful." Civil activism started with our first protest, the highly regarded Boston Tea Party, which was not a party. It was the colonists' protest against the Tea Act and taxation without representation.

Sinful conduct is such a serious matter that Scripture leaves no doubt about what relationship to have with those who foster conflict and division. Watch them, warn them, avoid them (see Romans 16:17-18, 1 Thessalonians 5:12-14, 2 Thessalonians 3:6-15). Also, Scripture tells us not to fellowship with the bad actors because it will corrupt our character. "Do not be misled. Bad company corrupts good character" (1 Corinthians 15:33). Scripture further sheds light on the contamination of fellowshipping with bad company in Galatians 5: "A little yeast works through the whole batch of dough" (Galatians 5:9). It extends to every group. "Righteousness exalts a nation, but sin is a disgrace to any people" (Proverbs 14:34 NASB). Authentic Christians can bring light and unity to the world.

> You are the salt of the earth. But if the salt loses its saltiness, how can it be made salty again? It is no longer good for anything except to be thrown out and trampled underfoot. You are the light of the world. A town built on a hill cannot

be hidden. Neither do people light a lamp and put it under a bowl. Instead, they put it on its stand, and it gives light to everyone in the house. In the same way, let your light shine before others, that they may see your good deeds and glorify your Father in heaven (Matthew 5:13-16).

Though Christians can make a difference, God alone gets the glory for good works. It is He who works progressive growth in Christians lives. Scripture tells us how to fix matters: "If my people, who are called by my name, will humble themselves and pray and seek my face and turn from their wicked ways, then I will hear from heaven, and I will forgive their sin and will heal their land" (2 Chronicles 7:14). Our recurring divisive battles will ultimately bring one result. "Implode within because of sin." We approached it on January 6, 2021.

CHAPTER 14

EXPERIENCES AND SOCIOECONOMICS

L ife experiences are part of us and shape us. Childhood experiences in particular shape who we become. Interactions with parents, siblings, and grandparents all impact us. Arguments, abusive or peaceful experiences in the home color who we become. Outside influences like teachers and others also affect us. Did you come from a loving home, or did you feel isolated and alone?

FAMILY EXPERIENCES DIFFERENCES

I include birth family with changeable differences because though you cannot change your birth family, you might not be reared by your birth family. Though family experiences have an impact on you, they do not have to define you. God can use all experiences to grow you. Psychology has long recognized that life experiences are part of what shapes who we become. Many receive counseling due to childhood and other experiences. Interactions with parents, siblings, grandparents, teachers, and neighbors all have an impact.

Reflect. What was your childhood experience? Hostile? Peaceful? Did you feel safe? Even our birth order has a role in shaping us.[19] The oldest child is more likely to be a leader. The second child bounces off the first child and gets their identity from being unlike the first child to the parents. We've heard about the middle child, the forgotten child, who struggles to gain the parents' attention. Because of the youngest child's attention, that child may become entitled and later angry when people don't give attention or meet their needs. These differences brought about by birth order clash within and outside the family. We can use these situations to learn to allow for the differences of others.

Multiple life event stressors also shape us like debt, finances, death of a loved one, childhood trauma. Experiences can also cause a filter through which we see situations that impact how we interact with others. With some experiences, you may develop defensive mechanisms or coping skills that carry. Role models play a part, whether excellent or poor. We see children have angry outbursts, modeling parents who have angry outbursts. We do not know what causes people's behavior, but we can accept people as valuable human beings and apply biblical principles to diverse encounters.

Robert Gill Gates depicts his family and societal heritage in his book *How Starbucks Saved My Life*. Gates grew up in wealth and privilege. As a boy, he and a young friend were rude to an older gentleman in Gates's father's presence. His father thought the behavior was humorous, whereas some parents would have corrected the child. His father's response to the behavior reinforced poor behavior.

As an adult, Gates lost his high-paying job of prestige and status and ended up homeless. He eventually got a job at Starbucks, where he worked with people whose existence he would not have previously noticed. At Starbucks, Gates learned your identity does not depend on external trappings but on who you are on the inside. He also learned how to treat others with respect and dignity. Gates's prior treatment of those he considered lower class based on economics was fertile ground for conflict. Yet, he learned to embrace differences and grew in character. The title of his book gives insight into his growth. Though we do not choose our families or experiences, we can change our behavior when we follow biblical principles in stewarding conflict. Like Gates, we learn to embrace differences, learn, and grow to bring unity.

SOCIOECONOMIC DIFFERENCES

Another difference is socioeconomic status, the social standing of an individual or group generally measured as a combination of income and occupation. Treating people differently because of different socioeconomic status can result in conflict. As Gates learned, such does not define who we are. Respect for people of different socioeconomic status can help you grow.

We can judge others based on outward appearance. Pastor Jack Wellman tells the story when he went up to a biker wearing a leather jacket with earrings and tattoos to share the gospel to lead the man to Christ. He states shame came over him when he learned the man was already saved. "But the Lord said to Samuel, 'Do not consider his appearance or his height, for I have rejected him. The Lord does not look at the things people do. People look at the outward appearance, but the Lord looks at the heart'" (1 Samuel 16:7). John 7:24 sheds further light: "Stop judging by mere appearances, but instead judge correctly" (John 7:24).

God created vast changeable and unchangeable differences. We are complex and have an intricate design. God can use our differences to grow us through the trials and conflict clashes. When we are refined through the fire to remove impurities, we become like Christ. Then our hearts, attitudes, and actions reflect Him. Our diversity rub clashes give us needed trials to practice godliness. Every fool will quarrel and vent, but the wise holds back (see Proverbs 20:3, Proverbs 29:11). Differences are not the problem; the heart's condition is the problem.

BIBLICAL PERSPECTIVE
OF THE RICH AND POOR

Solomon warns about the dangers of the love of money. "Whoever loves money never has enough; whoever loves wealth is never satisfied with their income. This too is meaningless" (Ecclesiastes 5:10). Paul agrees. Those who want to get rich fall into temptation and a trap and into many foolish and harmful desires that plunge people into ruin and destruction. Finally, Jesus had warned His disciple to beware of covetousness or greed (Luke 12:15).

The Bible also speaks against favoring the rich over the poor and refers to it as sin. (See James 2:9.) A *Harvard Business Review* article, "The Price of Wall Street's Power," shares that Wall Street intentionally makes decisions they know are wrong to influence governmental policies, including after a financial crisis. Upton Sinclair said in the article, "It is difficult to get a man to understand something when his salary depends on not understanding it." The result can be an entire society twisted to serve the interests of its most powerful group, further increasing that group's power in a vicious cycle.

The Bible tells us that while looking out for ourselves, we should also look out for the welfare of others (see Philippians 2:4). It takes an intentional effort. The body of Christ is one body, regardless of family or economic status. Brothers and sisters in Christ. "Do not think of yourself more highly than you ought, but rather think of yourself with sober judgment, in accordance with the faith God is distributed to each of you" (Romans 12:3).

The Bible's position on wealth differs from culture. Society highly esteems people based on wealth, often ignoring other factors. God does not respect the rich any more than the poor. It is our heart for Him that He respects. Three examples follow regarding riches.

THE RICH MAN AND POOR MAN LAZARUS

Scripture does not view the rich and poor in the same way as the culture. Scripture tells us the parable of the rich man and the poor man Lazarus. While on earth the rich man had all the world's finest of everything, whereas poor man Lazarus sought to eat crumbs that fell from the rich man's table. Both died. The roles were then reversed. The rich man went to hell, where he lived in torment. Lazarus went to heaven, where he lived in comfort (see Luke 16:19-31). The rich man could see Lazarus in heaven and asked if Lazarus could merely dip his finger in water and come cool the rich man's tongue, but it was too late. What was the rich man's crime? Certainly, not being rich. However, he loved his riches and made poor use of them, not even having regard for a poor beggar wanting to eat what fell from his table (see Luke 16:19-31).

You can have monetary wealth and be poor. "You say, 'I am rich; I have acquired wealth and do not need a thing.' But you do not realize that you are wretched, pitiful, poor, blind and naked" (Revelation 3:17).

THE WIDOW'S GIFT OFFERING

Scripture tells a story of a poor widow's gift to the church. The affluent put in large sums of money, while the poor widow put in a coin worth less than a penny, but it was everything she had. Jesus told the disciples that the poor widow put in more than anyone else—she gave all she had. Jesus, who watched them put in their money, told the disciples the widow gave more than the others (see Mark 12:42–44). She not only gave proportionally more, but her giving reflected her heart and trust in God when she gave her all.

THE RICH FOOL

We need money, but we are more valuable than our money. While growing money, don't forget to grow yourself—your character, love for others, and love for God. Luke 12 tells the parable of the rich man who had such an abundance he had to build bigger barns to store all his wealth and then take it easy for the rest of his life and have fun, not knowing that God would call him a fool and tell him he would die that night (see Luke 12:13-2). Again, the problem was not his riches but his lack of richness toward God. The Bible does not state that money is evil, but the love of money is evil (see 1 Timothy 6:10).

Also be mindful that wealth gained appropriately should be enjoyed and used as God directs, however, wealth gained by evil means will boomerang back to impact you adversely. "These men lie in wait for their own blood; they ambush only themselves! Such are the paths of all who go after ill-gotten gain; it takes away the life of those who get it" (Proverbs 1:18-19). Riches don't make a person evil, and poverty does not make a person righteous. It is always the condition of the heart. Whatever the status, neither should think of themselves more highly than they should. We obtain bigger homes and finer cars, travel and live a life of fun. That is great, we should enjoy the fruit of our labor, but what about the spiritual aspect of our lives. While we are growing our money, let's grow ourselves. God can use our differences to grow us when our hearts, attitudes, and actions reflect Him.

PERSONAL PREFERENCES DIFFERENCES

Personal preference differences speak for themselves. Like personality clashes and other differences, personal preferences can bring clashes. The same analogy applies. We can handle it constructively or destructively. One leads to peace and growth, the other leads to conflict.

SOCIAL JUSTICE

Society measures social justice by looking at the balance of distribution of wealth's impact on civil liberties, equal opportunity, taxation, health access, and education. Sociologist Alexes Harris of the University of Washington found an investigation revealed that indigents are financially unable to navigate the legal system due to finances and face harsher treatment than others who can pay court costs.

God is never unjust. He loves righteousness and justice. "The LORD loves righteousness and justice" (Psalm 33:5). His divine governance is based on righteousness and justice. As stated in Psalm 89, "Righteousness and justice are the foundation of your throne; love and faithfulness go before you" (Psalm 89:14). The two are coupled and based on God's Word. "Righteousness is the moral standard of right and wrong to which God holds men accountable based on His divine standard. Justice is equitable and impartial application of God's moral law in society."[20]

CHAPTER 15

RESPONSES TO CONFLICT

People respond to conflict in various ways, which can bring diversity clashes that give us the opportunity to practice biblical principles to grow. Though we can respond in any manner depending on the situation, everyone has a dominant mode of response to conflict. Reflect regarding people you know and note how they respond to conflict differently.

In this chapter, we will first define and describe the general categories of response to conflict and how different personalities respond to conflict. Finally, we will describe how one's level of spiritual maturity impacts the response to conflict.

THREE TYPES OF RESPONSES TO CONFLICT

There are three dominant responses to conflict. In *The Peacemaker*, Ken Sande, the founder of Peacemaker Ministries and Relational Wisdom 360, categorizes the responses as escape, attack, and conciliation. I think of them as flight, fight, or do right. Each category has subcategories to which I refer you to Sande's book. The way we respond to conflict can promote or heighten a clash. The chief aim of life is to bring God glory. We bring Him glory when we grow spiritually. We can grow through clashing responses to conflict. Like refining sugar brings the byproduct of molasses, spiritual growth also brings the byproduct of love, peace, and unity.

Escape Responses

If you tend to avoid conflict, your dominant mode of response to conflict is to escape the conflict. The escape responder focuses on protecting oneself by getting away from the other person and the battle. There are times when fleeing conflict is the desired response, like in the case of danger. We see another wise escape in Genesis 12:7, where Joseph ran from Potiphar's wife. "She caught him by his cloak and said, 'Come to bed with me!' But he left his cloak in her hand and ran out of the house" (Genesis 39:12). But sometimes, we need to stay with a conversation rather than escaping, like the case of a marital disagreement that requires attention.

Attack Responses

Those inclined toward fighting in response to conflict have attack as their dominant mode of response to conflict. The attack person's focus is on harming the other person to resolve the dispute. I had a former co-worker who was an attack responder who usually initiated a fight. She had a reputation of needing to fight with someone at all times. It got so bad that management disciplined her. It got better afterward, but then the office joke became, "She can't keep up the nice façade. Just wait; she's gonna crack." Despite the employee's natural inclination, the way we respond to conflict is a changeable difference. Real change comes from within through character growth.

An attack example is when the Sanhedrin stoned Stephen to death (see Acts 7:54-60). Another example of an attack response to conflict is found in 1 Samuel when Saul tried to stab David with a spear. "Saul had a spear in his hand and he hurled it, saying to himself, 'I'll pin David to the wall'... But David eluded him twice" (1 Samuel 18:10-11). Note that Saul's behavior was attack and David's was escape.

Conciliation Responses

If you are inclined toward peaceful resolution of conflict, your primary mode of response to conflict is conciliation. Conciliatory responses focus on the interest of both parties. That is one way to serve as a minister of reconciliation. "Do nothing from selfish ambition or conceit, but in humility count others more significant than yourselves. Let each of you look not only to his own interests, but also to the interests of others" (Philippians 2:3-4 ESV).

DIFFERING RESPONSES BASED ON PERSONALITY

Based on our personality, we react differently under pressure and have different sources of irritation. Every personality type has a sensitive spot or hot button for conflict.[21] Different personalities act differently when under pressure or when irritated. I give broad general information on how the personalities act under pressure and what irritates each type leading to conflict. These naturally arising behaviors provide the opportunity to interact with differences and apply biblical principles for character development.

The supportive "S" personality becomes insecure under pressure and is irritated by inflexibility.

The critical "C" personality who is motivated by correctness becomes moody under pressure and gets annoyed over incompetence. The take-charge, controlling "D" personality becomes dictatorial under pressure and vexed by weakness and indecisiveness. The people-person, life of the party "I" personality becomes hyper and overly optimistic under pressure. They are irritated by pessimism and doubt. No matter how one naturally operates under pressure or their sources of irritation, resisting wrongdoing and submitting to God will help them overcome.

SPIRITUAL MATURITY AS A CONFLICT MANAGEMENT INDICATOR

Because our level of spiritual maturity differs, our capacity to manage conflict will also vary. All believers start as baby Christians who are not mature to resolve disputes. Encourage reconciliation, but don't force reconciliation. Peace is a matter of the heart. That is why forced reconciliation is not genuine. Everyone does not have the same tenderness of heart for peace.

We manage conflict in direct proportion to our spiritual maturity. My first degree was a Bachelor of Science in mathematics. In mathematics, direct proportion theory states that when one variable changes, the other changes in direct proportion to the first variable's change. When the first variable goes up, the other variable goes up. The same when the variable goes down. In applying the direct portion theory to peacemaking, the variables are spiritual maturity and conflict resolution. When our spiritual maturity goes up, our conflict resolution skills go up. The more mature we are, the greater our capacity to manage conflict. The less mature we are, the lesser the ability to handle conflict.

In maturity, we become more like Christ, wherein our ability to manage conflict improves. That is why it is imperative to strengthen your conflict resolution muscles by practicing biblical principles during differences clashes. Personal trainers teach us that strength training enhances our physical body and gives our muscles more power. We gain muscle gradually as we increase the weight to work the muscles harder. Likewise, our spiritual growth is gradual. We exercise the muscles in repetition for progress. We do not become skilled at conflict resolution from one victory. We gain greater heights and move progressively up the spiritual maturity ladder as we manage more difficult struggles in life.

In strength training, form is crucial. Slow controlled movements are required for muscle tension to avoid injury. Likewise, in conflict resolution, you must control yourself and speak gently to turn away anger (see Proverbs 15:1). We widely recognize the benefits of strength training and other exercises that build our core. Do no less for our spiritual well-being than we do for the physical body. "For physical training is of some value, but godliness has value for all things, holding promise for both the present life and the life to come" (1 Timothy 4:8).

Note the maturity level of the person with whom you are in conflict and act accordingly. "We who are strong ought to bear with the failings of the weak and not to please ourselves" (Romans 15:1). Otherwise, we will choke a spiritual baby to death by giving them steak reconciliation when they can only take in milk reconciliation. Do not judge or condemn them. Bear with, forgive, and love them (See Ephesians 4:1-4). They make the decision generally based on their capacity to manage conflict. Whatever their decision, God is their judge and ours. Pray for one another. Allow for differences of opinions and reactions.

FORCED RECONCILIATION

A person tried to force reconciliation among two groups in conflict due to differences in viewpoints, but it did not work. All the people love God, but both sides judged and had negative interpretations of the other side. Sometimes based on the nature of the conflict and the hurts involved, it may take time. You can encourage people, but true reconciliation comes from the heart. Trying to control or manipulate a resolution is pushing your choice over the free will that God gave them.

CONFLICT MANAGEMENT CAPACITY

People can come with peace-breaking baggage, which lead to responses that provoke division and strife. The below categories of conflict management capacity are based on differing levels of spiritual maturity. "Desire(s)" peace in the categories refers to having a heart for peace. The categories are general in nature because based on the egregiousness of an offense and a person's emotional state at the time, a different response can occur. We are not mechanical beings.

Conflict Management Capable—desires peace and able to work positively toward conflict resolution. This person is spiritually mature and generally acts righteously. However, no person is perfect and can miss the mark periodically.

Conflict Management Capable with Support—desires peace, but at times may need conflict coaching support to resolve conflict. Feelings can be raw and conflicted parties may need a neutral third party to assist them. A mediator is a go-between to assist the parties. As ministers of reconciliation, we can serve as mediators to help others resolve the matter. Christ is the mediator between God and us, "For there is one God and one mediator between God and mankind, the man Christ Jesus" (1 Timothy 2:5).

Conflict Management Capable with Limitations—desires peace but struggles during interactions with others. This person can often be helped in several ways; mediation, training, heightened awareness of need to obey God, and spiritual growth.

Conflict Management Incapable at this Time—does not desire peace. Appears to thrive in chaos, unwilling or unable to resolve conflict. The person may be so wounded or so spiritually immature or unspiritual they need time. Pray for them and model the way.

Recognize the different capacities for managing conflict and allow for differences. Allow God to work in other people's lives, as He works in yours. We sin when we spiritually choke less mature Christians. Babies first learn how to crawl, then walk, and then run for peaceful conflict resolution. If we are more mature spiritually, we can demonstrate patience with others and help them. If we are not doing so, perhaps we are not as spiritually mature as we believe. What if you want to make peace and they don't? Romans 12:18 encourages us, "If it is possible, as far as it depends on you, live at peace with everyone."

HUMILITY

Conflict management requires humility. Some people are full of pride and arrogance, thinking more highly of themselves than they should (see Romans 12:3). Humility is the opposite of pride. Matthew 5:3 describes humility: "Blessed are the poor in spirit, for theirs is the kingdom of heaven." One who is poor in spirit acknowledges spiritual poorness in need of dependence on God. Note the special blessing for those who are humble, a place in the Kingdom of heaven. Indeed, humility is required for the work God calls us to perform. "For we are God's handiwork, created in Christ Jesus to do good works, which God prepared in advance for us to do" (Ephesians 2:19). Humility gives us wisdom and honor (see Proverbs 11:2, 22:4).

CHAPTER 16

OUR SAMENESS: COMMON GROUND FOR UNITY

I praise you because I am fearfully and wonderfully made;
your works are wonderful, I know that full well.

PSALM 139:14

THE WONDER OF HUMANITY

The Seven Wonders of the Ancient World and the many natural wonders worldwide are marvelous to behold, but none of them is as great a wonder as you. Who are we that God is mindful of us? He gave us dignity by creating us in His image and a little lower than the angels and gave us the world to rule (see Psalm 8:4-6, Genesis 1:27). We are God's children and co-heirs with Christ, "if indeed we share in his sufferings in order that we may also share in his glory" (Romans 8:16-17). He also likens us to sheep in His world pasture. Psalm 100:3 (KJV) says, "Know ye that the LORD, He is God; it is He that hath made us, and not we ourselves. We are His people, and the sheep of His pasture."

The complexity of humanity is incredible. God made us in His image and gave us will, intellect, and emotion. He gave us five senses to send stimuli to the brain to understand and perceive the world. Our human body systems are a wonderment; respiratory, circulatory, digestive system, nervous system, urinary system, skeletal, and muscular system. The psalmist recognized the majesty of God's creation in humanity: "I praise you because I am fearfully and wonderfully made; your works are wonderful, I know that full well" (Psalm 139:14). We have our humanity in common. He created us as social beings for family units and believers' community relationships within complex society.

YOU ARE VALUABLE

We may have different perceptions, interests, and motivations, but we also have sameness. Differences tend to divide us, whereas things we have in common can unite us if we permit it. One common characteristic is that we are all valuable. I once saw a man's silhouette in a magazine with the silhouette filled in with newspaper print. Something bothered me about the image. I soon realized that it was because it depicted the man as merely another news story. We all have a story, but we are much more than a news story. We are the highest creation made by God. The fact that He made us in His image is evidence of our value. Christ dying for us further proves our value. You do not die for something worthless. Our value never changes, though we may feel low periodically or act beneath who we are. Our value is intrinsic, not based on performance or feelings. Nothing can change the fact that God made us in His image, and Christ died for us. We need not try to bend others to our image or our preferences. They are as intrinsically valuable as any other.

Valuables are treated differently from non-valuables. How do you treat something of value? With care. As I shared earlier, I have a few things that my mom gave me when she was living. I treat them with care because of their value to me. One of the items is an old, stained linen handkerchief. That old linen handkerchief came to me in a special way that is too detailed to tell here. I imagine no one would give me a nickel for it in a garage sale, yet it is precious to me. It reminds me of the love between mother and daughter and the fact that she valued me. When I look at it, I feel good! When we treat people as valuable, it meets a basic human need and generally brings a positive result. I go back to my reference in an earlier chapter of Abraham Maslow's hierarchy of human needs pyramid. His pyramid shows the need to be esteemed high on the hierarchal chart of human needs. We have a normal desire to be valued and treated with respect and dignity. Whether it is diversity or other encounters, treat people with respect and dignity. It is a righteous action, and it curtails conflict. Every person is more valuable than the most valuable material good anyone owns.

The humanity in us recognizes the humanity in others. I find it difficult to imagine anyone can see another human being suffering or hurting without feeling compassion. One lady said she witnessed a stranger fall so hard that he hit his head with a loud bang on the pavement. She started crying out because the sound led her to believe that he was seriously injured. Human dignity is shown by the Good Samaritan helping the injured man on the roadside. It was humanity on the side of the road, not a piece of trash. God's commandment not to kill further shows how we are to respect human life. However, we can also kill with our words. False words are a weapon that wounds. "Like a club or a sword or a sharp arrow is one who gives false testimony against a neighbor" (Proverbs 25:18). When we harm others, it includes harm to ourselves and society. No one wins in wrongdoing.

OUR UNIQUENESS

Another sameness of our humanity is that we are each unique. That sounds contradictory since uniqueness implies distinctiveness. Even though our uniqueness distinguishes us from others, we are the same in that we are each unique. I heard a sermon years ago about God being so unique that everything He makes is original. The preacher said each of us is unique. God is so unique that nothing He makes is the same. No two snowflakes, no two leaves, not even two chinaberries are the same. I did not know the meaning of a chinaberry, but I got his point. Each person is unique. An original has a higher value than a copy, and we are each original. As an original, no one can be you but you. God brought each person into the world with a unique purpose that no one else can fulfill the way that person can. When we act righteously and allow for the differences of others, it works toward fulfilling our purpose and letting others fulfill their purpose.

The world has made great strides in science relating to DNA. God created us so uniquely that our individual DNA can identify us. Law enforcement identifies perpetrators of crime or determines parentage from DNA. You are one of a kind for God's designed plan. You have much to offer to your family, friends, and society. Only you can bring peacemaking and unity to certain situations.

Russell Kelfer's poem, "You Are Who You Are for a Reason" describes our uniqueness. I provide a paraphrase of a portion of the poem here. He ordained and foreknew who our parents would be, how we would look, and allowed us to go through experiences for growth. Though painful, He superintended every growth experience.

We are clay that God creatively formed into pottery as He saw fit. "Yet you, LORD, are our Father. We are the clay, you are the potter; we are all the work of your hand" (Isaiah 64:8). From the first birth to the present, God foreknew us and formed us in our mother's womb and had a plan for creating each of us (See Jeremiah 1:5; Psalm 139:13).

EVERYBODY IS SOMEBODY

God so loves us that He sent Christ to die for us. Lift your heads from being downcast. In recognition that the God of the universe is mindful of you and has a plan for you. That is a sameness element for all humanity. Each person matters. In God's sight, we are all the same. "There is neither Jew nor Gentile, neither slave nor free, nor is there male and female, for you are all one in Christ Jesus" (Galatians 3:28). We get our value from the fact that God made us in His image. As Ethel Waters has said, "I am somebody cause God don't make no junk."

That is a good foundation from which to be mindful when you interact with others. We are all in the same boat of humanity. Each person has common life issues and problems; relationship issues, grief from losing a loved one, financial management concerns, possible self-esteem issues, illness, job issues, etc.

Everybody is somebody, and other people are somebody. We make judgements and decisions based on a person's status. Status is how we rank people according to societal rules related to a person's money, profession, or class, generally associated with wealth or lack thereof. In summary, we are in the same boat of life, all made in God's image. We are sinners saved by God's grace and for whom Christ died. We have our true identity in Him, not material things. If you profess Christ, you have the same daddy as others who profess Christ, family members in one family. Accepting everyone as valuable is part of our spiritual growth and can bring more peace and unity.

We give God praise because His name is the most majestic name on earth (See Psalm 8:1). Composer George Friedrich Handel composed the "Hallelujah Chorus," still a renowned piece today. Handel, a devout Christian, used text from the Bible for the work. One of the background stories related to the work alleges that the music so touched King George II, he stood, which automatically caused all his subjects to stand. In some countries, people still stand at the singing of the "Hallelujah Chorus." I have not heard the Hallelujah Chorus in many years, but I recall standing for it as a child in school and church. Most of the song is a repeated frame of the word *hallelujah* in artful rising and falling musical crescendo and decrescendo. There is no wonder King George II stood up for the song's words that also include "King of Kings and Lord of Lords" (Revelation 19:15). Humanity is a wonder, but no human is as great a wonder as God. We breathe because of Him. He made the universe and everything in it.

PART 5

RESOLUTION POWER

CHAPTER 17

RESOLUTION LAND: A MINDSET

*The mind governed by the flesh is death, but the
mind governed by the Spirit is life and peace.*

ROMANS 8:6

What does God want from us? He does not leave us ignorant. He tells us throughout the Bible. Here are examples.

- He created us for His glory (See Isaiah 43:7, 1 Corinthians 10:31).

- He made us to do good works, "For we are God's handiwork, created in Christ Jesus to do good works, which God prepared in advance for us to do" (Ephesians 2:10).

- He created us for Himself and desires that we seek His strength and presence continually (see Colossians 1:16, 1 Chronicles 16:11, Psalm 105:4).

- He desires that we be righteous and holy (see Ephesians 4:24).

Thus, He created us to honor Him by living righteous lives through service to Him and others. In short, He desires to rule every aspect of our lives. Allowing Him to do so can only benefit us.

LIVING IN COMMUNITY

The ongoing pursuit of peace and harmony is what I refer to as living in "Resolution Land." Resolution Land is a mindset and attitude that brings peacemaking action. "The mind governed by the flesh is death, but the mind governed by the Spirit is life and peace. The mind governed by the flesh is hostile to God; it does not submit to God's law, nor can it do so" (Romans 8:6-7). In Resolution Land, you have purposed in your heart, made up your mind, and are determined to pursue peaceful relationships in obedience to God. It is a way of thinking that leads to action that fosters harmony in relationships.

God designed us to live in community. Living in community does not refer to a geographical location as in a residential district or local neighborhood. It refers to how the body of Christ needs to interrelate with one another. We grow in community when we interact with others. Living in authentic community is characterized by loving care for one another in a righteous, God-honoring way. Loving care is a foundational principle to resolve conflict. God instructs us to love one another for people to know we belong to Him (See John 13:35). We are supposed to show love not merely by what we say but also by our actions (See 1 John 3:18). In Resolution Land, people living in Christian community understand the benefit and power of

- God's Word
- The Holy Spirit
- Displaying love and grace
- Forgiveness
- Confession

GOD'S WORD

The Bible instructs us on how to live. It is impossible to live in Resolution Land, where you have a mindset to pursue peace without God's Word. The Bible is sufficient for living in every avenue of life. God's

Word is distinctive, "For the word of God is alive and active. Sharper than any double-edged sword, it penetrates even to dividing soul and spirit, joints and marrow; it judges the thoughts and attitudes of the heart" (Hebrews 4:12). By partial interpretation, God's Word is actively alive. It is so sharp, it cuts like a "two-edged" sword and pierces through to man's soul, where hidden feelings and thoughts reside. It is with God's Word that we can renew our minds from sinful thoughts to righteous thoughts (see Romans 12:2). The Word is like rain that falls to fulfill God's purpose. If we had no rain, we would have no food. Plants need rain to grow so we can have food to sustain life. Like rain fulfills its purpose, God's Word fulfills its purpose. We need it for life.

> As the rain and the snow come down from heaven, and do not return to it without watering the earth and making it bud and flourish, so that it yields seed for the sower and bread for the eater, so is my Word that goes out from my mouth: It will not return to me empty, but will accomplish what I desire and achieve the purpose for which I sent it (Isaiah 55:10-11).

God's Word lights the way through the dark paths of life, so that we see the right direction to go. "Your word is a lamp for my feet, a light on my path" (Psalm 119:105). Moreover, the written word (Scripture) helps us know the Living Word, Jesus. After salvation, I started reading the Bible. It was difficult. I struggled with understanding. I did not know that I was a baby in Christ. I read one chapter and did not understand much of it. I started reading 3-5 verses daily, or less. I was excited to gain understanding when I meditated on just a few verses at a time. Reading the Bible is not an intellectual feat, it is a spiritual experience wherein the Holy Spirit illuminates the Word, and turns on the light of your understanding. Over time, I could understand more verses, then chapters, then books of the Bible and then the Bible, God's love story to us through Jesus. Do not be discouraged if it is difficult for you to understand God's Word. You gain and understand more as you grow.

God's Word stirred the hearts of the disciples, who talked about how their hearts burned when Jesus opened up the Scriptures to them.

"Were not our hearts burning within us while he talked with us on the road and opened the scriptures to us?" (Luke 24:32). Scripture nourishes us spiritually like food nourishes the body. "We don't live by bread alone but by every Word that proceeds out of the mouth of the Lord Jesus Christ" (Matthew 4:4). God's Word educates us and is light on the dark paths of life so we can see the right way to go (see Psalm 119: 105). It reveals the mysteries of life (Job 12:22, Daniel 2:22, Jeremiah 33:3).

How can we remember the vastness of all the Scriptures in the Bible? One of the miraculous things about salvation is that God gives us the Holy Spirit, His Spirit, at the point of salvation. The Holy Spirit brings to our remembrance Scriptures we need at the precise moment of need for us to act righteously. Scripture tells us to study God's Word so that we can be accurate when we share and apply the Word (See 2 Timothy 2:15). We need God's Word in us so that the Holy Spirit can bring it to remembrance. Of course, we can't remember what we never knew. Even so, the Holy Spirit even guides if we do not know Scripture related to the issue. He provides insight the human conscience cannot provide. When we learn His Word, we can hide it in our hearts to keep from sin. "I have hidden your word in my heart that I might not sin against you" (Psalm 119:11). We can experience the tasty savor of a relationship with God. "Taste and see that the LORD is good; blessed is the one who takes refuge in him" (Psalm 34:8).

WHO IS THE HOLY SPIRIT

God is three Persons in one; God the Father, God the Son, and God the Holy Spirit. We refer to the three as the Holy Trinity. The Holy Spirit is a divine Person with the three characteristics of personhood:

- Will (see 1 Corinthians 12:11),
- Intellect (see 1 Corinthians 2:10-11), and
- Emotion (see Ephesians 4:3).

The Holy Spirit helps us live in unity in Resolution Land. He is the promise of Jesus to the disciples that He would send a Helper. "But you will receive power when the Holy Spirit comes on you; and you will be my witnesses in Jerusalem, and in all Judea and Samaria, and to the ends of the earth" (Acts 1:8). In life's journey, we need the Holy Spirit's power to help us live righteously through encounters and witness to others. When we encounter conflict, we can feel intimidated, but the Holy Spirit empowers us. The Greek word for power is *dunamis*, which is the same power that raised Jesus from the dead. That power also lives in us (see Romans 8:11). We can lovingly confront those with whom we have conflict. There is nothing to fear because God did not put fear in us but power. "For the Spirit God gave us does not make us timid, but gives us power, love and self-discipline" (2 Timothy 1:7).

THE HOLY SPIRIT HELPS US

We have the greatest power on earth within us. Unfortunately, we do not recognize or do not use the power we have. That leaves us operating from a position of weakness. The Holy Spirit does the following for us:

- empowers us (Acts 1:8),

- indwells us (Romans 5:5, 8:9; 2 Corinthians 5:5),

- seals us until the day of redemption (2 Corinthians 1:22, Ephesians1:13-14),

- brings things to remembrance (John 14:26),

- guides us (Romans 8:14, Galatians 5:18),

- illuminates and teaches spiritual truth (John 14:26, 16:12-15, 1 Corinthians 2:9-16),

- sanctifies by applying Christ's righteousness to us (2 Corinthians 3:18),

- convicts of sin (John 16:7-11),

- and indwells us (1 Corinthians 3:16, 1 Corinthians 6:19, 2 Timothy 1:14).

We can grieve and quench the Holy Spirit. We can also yield to the Spirit, be filled with the Spirit, and walk by the Spirit, each explained below.

The *Filling of the Holy Spirit* is true spirituality reflected in the God-honoring quality of the believer's life of victory and power over sin. We become filled based on our habitual, ongoing yielding to Christ such that we come under the control of the Spirit. We then become an instrument of righteousness for service rather than an instrument for ungodly behavior.[22]

The *Grieving of the Spirit* brings about the emotion of hurt to the Spirit by our failure to live in unity. We especially grieve the Holy Spirit with disunity caused by our yielding to the flesh to speak unwholesome words that destroy relationships and bring disharmony in the body rather than build up the body.[23]

The *Quenching of the Spirit* is a believer consciously not yielding to the prompting of the Holy Spirit in disobedience to God's scripturally revealed Word. It is when we intentionally hinder, restrict, resist, or counteract the influence of God's Spirit in rebellion against God. We refuse to depend on Him but instead rely on the flesh.[24]

Yielding to the Spirit is willingness to surrender to whatever the will of God is in the believer's life by trusting God through the role of the indwelling Holy Spirit to will and do His good pleasure rather than yielding to the flesh of independence from God.[25]

Walking by the Spirit is maintaining an attitude of relying and depending on God's provision of the Holy Spirit day to day; for guidance and power not to fill the sinful desires of the flesh but continue to draw on the maintenance of the Spirit's control.[26]

The Ethical Concept of the Flesh includes both the physical body and the moral meaning related to the whole unregenerate natural man of sinful impulses and desires. The physical body is the instrument through which sin expresses itself.[27] The Bible specifically provides examples of fleshly behavior. "The acts of the flesh are obvious: sexual immorality, impurity and debauchery; idolatry and witchcraft; hatred, discord, jealousy, fits of rage, selfish ambition, dissensions, factions" (Galatians 5:19-20). The flesh's ethical concept's moral meaning relates to our depraved, naturally sinful impulses and desires. We carry out sin in our thoughts, words, and actions through the physical body. We hear people say certain behaviors are walking in the flesh rather than walking in the Spirit.

SUMMARY: THE HOLY SPIRIT

With the filling of the Spirit, we yield to the Spirit and allow the Spirit to control our behavior. It gives us the power to walk by the Spirit and draw on the Spirit's control rather than fulfill the flesh's sinful desires. Because the Holy Spirit is in us, He convicts us of sin. The Spirit prompts us to do right when choices present themselves to us, but we pain the Spirit when we willingly stifle and quench the Spirit's prompting rather than surrendering to His prompting. People often quench the Spirit in conflict and operate out of control, yielding to the flesh to perform acts that bring disunity. Our thwarting of the Spirit's prompting is sinful rebellion against God. We need help; we have a Helper, but often lean and depend only on our weak natural strength instead of the Holy Spirit's supernatural, powerful strength. We can use the help God provided us for the purpose provided. We cannot live in peace and harmony without the aid of the Holy Spirit. Successful living in Resolution Land also requires a humble heart.

Humility
(Proverbs 16:18; Acts 10:34)

We are nobody when we think we are somebody, separate and apart from Christ.

We are no better than the poor, the unschooled,
the illiterate in life.

Humble yourself and be respectful to all.
For pride and arrogance, there is no call.

Keep it up if you will,
You're cruising for a big fall.

Humble yourself and be lifted up.
Lift yourself up and go down for messing up.

GRACE

Grace is God's favor to us that we do not deserve and cannot earn.
He gives grace to everyone, but more particularly His children. In *The
Grace Awakening*, Chuck Swindoll states that grace not only changes
our heart, but it also changes our faces.[28] He tells the story of men having to ford a dangerous stream of water on horseback. A man stood on
the ground watching the men on horseback. When some of the men
had safely made it across to the other side, the man asked President
Thomas Jefferson if he would take him across on Jefferson's horse. The
President immediately said "yes."

The man hopped on behind the President, and they safely crossed
the dangerous water. When they had gotten safely to the other side,
one of the men asked him why he had selected the President to ask
for help. The man stated he did not know it was the President. He
said, all I know is that some of you had a "no" face, but the President
had a "yes" face. God's grace will change your countenance. When we
grasp grace, we become less petty-minded, and it frees us from bondage and fear of others. Be delivered from people and their opinions.
Don't let people put you in bondage, and don't put others in bondage. Grace will cause you to allow for the differences of others. "Love
that goes upward is worship; love that goes outward is affection; love
that stoops is grace" (Donald Barnhouse). God stoops down to our
level to clean us up.

FORGIVENESS

Forgiveness lives large in Resolution Land. The very foundation of our relationship with God is built on His forgiveness of our sins. Forgiveness is to pardon or release a person from an obligation they owe. That is what God did for us on Calvary. "But God demonstrates his own love for us in this: While we were still sinners, Christ died for us" (Romans 5:8). Our action or inaction of forgiveness is automatically reciprocated in God's universal system. "But if you do not forgive others their sins, your Father will not forgive your sins" (Matthew 6:15). The word grace (unmerited favor) is the root word for forgive. That is what Christ did for us; forgave us though we did not deserve it. That is what we should do for others; forgive though they might not deserve it. Corrie Ten Boom survived the Nazi concentration camp, where they killed her parents and sister. She said, "Forgiveness is to set a prisoner free, and to realize the prisoner is you."

A friend struggled with forgiving herself regarding a wrong she did over 20 years ago. She allowed the devil to bring mental harassment to her. Forgiveness also includes forgiving yourself. After repentance, let it go. Be mindful of resting in the provision of Romans 8:1 that there is no condemnation to those *in Christ Jesus* (emphasis added). Therefore, do not insist on feeling guilt when the finished work of Christ removed condemnation from us.

Family Forgiveness Story: We were devastated. Surely, it was a nightmare from which we would awake? But it was real. My nephew had been shot and killed. This happens in a horror movie, not in my family. Within a few weeks of his son's death, my brother told his wife, we must forgive. I marveled at my brother's resolve. My brother, who had lost his youngest son moved to the need to forgive. The devil wants us to have a heart of unforgiveness to harm us. When we fail to forgive, we play into his schemes against us. We can quote scriptures on forgiveness, but when the rubber meets the road on the hard cases, like my nephew's case, where do we stand? We can more easily forgive minor infractions, but what about the severe offenses perpetrated against us? In our fallen world of sin, we will always encounter the need to forgive or be forgiven because we sin against others and others sin against us. Your examples may not be as extreme as my nephew's killing, but on the other hand, it could be. Whatever the situation, always forgive. "But if you do not forgive others their sins, your Father will not forgive your sins" (Matthew 6:15).

Let it Go

Forgive says "Let it go!"
Or bitterness and resentment will flow,
Imprisoning the one who doesn't forgive.
Blocking freedom from within to live.

Jesus betrayed so many times,
Though He committed no crimes.
Yet, He showed absolutely no malice
Toward those whose hearts were callous.

Waste not our bones away,
Allowing unforgiveness to stay.
Forgive as Christ forgave,
Teaching us how to behave.

Holding on finds no peace,
But blocks us from the Lord's release
Yes, we ultimately must let go
If we want to be pardoned also.[29]

JEAN STUBBLEFIELD SIMS, USED BY PERMISSION

CONFESSION

In our restored relationship with God, we don't always get it right. God has graciously given us the provision of confessing our sins when we get it wrong. In Resolution Land, we immediately confess sin. "If we confess our sins, he is faithful and just and will forgive us our sins and purify us from all unrighteousness" (1 John 1:9).

One of the most notable confessions in the Bible is King David's lament in Psalm 51, after the prophet Nathan confronted him for having Uriah killed to hide his adultery with Uriah's wife, Bathsheba. She was pregnant and had not been with her husband. David thought he had covered up the sin of adultery and murder until God sent the prophet Nathan to confront him. Like David, we may think we can hide or get away with sin, but we can never hide sin from God. Sin is against God and separates us from Him. David paid consequences for his sin, and we pay consequences for our sin. Yet, David is a beautiful example of God's graciousness toward us when we repent.

In the natural sense, you wonder how this adulterous, murderous man could be a man after God's own heart, as described in 1 Samuel 13:14. Lest we judge too quickly, reflect and recall our own human sinfulness and depravity. Remember also, "for all have sinned and fall short of the glory of God" (Romans 3:23). David wrote the majority of the 150 Psalms. He loved God's Word, meditated, and delighted in it day and night (see Psalm 119:47-48). He sought to follow God yet sinned like all humans. What distinguished David was his practice of crying out to God and genuinely confessing his sinful acts. While David's story is an excellent example of confession because it illustrates authentic repentance, we each have our own stories of sin, confession, or lack of confession. That does not mean we should intentionally sin because we can ask God to forgive us. God forbid.

PERSONAL EXAMPLE OF CONFESSION AND FORGIVENESS

In Resolution Land, we confess and forgive. We all have a story. I tell one of my stories, though not my favorite story to tell. In fact, I don't like to tell it at all. I do so because it may help someone else. I wronged someone, but God graciously helped me out of my failure. We can have logs in our eyes. "You hypocrite, first take the plank out of your own eye, and then you will see clearly to remove the speck from your brother's eye" (Matthew 7:5). Relationships are important. God made us for relationships, evidenced by the two greatest commandments; fervently love God and love others as ourselves (see Matthew 22:36-40).

I am close to a Christian who got off on the wrong track. I got angry regarding her lifestyle, so I picked up the phone, verbally blasted her, and then hung up the phone. I was so out of order. The Holy Spirit immediately convicted me. When convicted of sin, I learned a long time ago, act immediately, or have no inner peace. I grabbed the phone, called her back, and asked her to forgive me because I had sinned against her. She started crying and said, "I want to get it right, but I am struggling."

It is wrong when people minister patiently to strangers or those they don't know well but seem impatient with loved ones. We tend to be more judgmental of family and friends. Perhaps it is because we care so much for them. Nonetheless, people don't need our judgment. When we go into the devil's territory, he grasps us, and it can be hard to shake loose, as she admitted about her struggles. She did not need my condemnation; she needed my love. She forgave me. She also overcame that sin. What I failed to realize when I condemned her is that I was no different from her. While I scolded her for sin, I sinned by condemning her.

Logs in our eyes blind us from clear sight. I had the anger and judgmental logs in my eye, where I could not see how to interact with her lovingly. Love helps and curtails conflict. That incident made her a better person, and it made me a better person. People need to know that we care, and they need to see God in us based on our loving behavior. But for God's grace, any of us will fall. "So, if you think you are standing firm, be careful that you don't fall" (1 Corinthians 10:12). My story with the person concludes with the fact that today, she is strong in God and faithfully serving Him.

PERSONAL EXAMPLE OF GETTING IT RIGHT

In Resolution Land, you serve as a minister of reconciliation to help others resolve conflict. A church in Texas contacted me to mediate a dispute among top leadership. I met with the group and held two mediations, which could not have turned out better. We had a real sense of community as we worked together to resolve the issue. During the mediation, they respected each other, allowed for differences, and used biblical principles to unify. That was the best case I ever mediated because it was clear that each of them wanted to biblically resolve the matter and please God. A genuine heart for peace is required, not the impossibility of perfection. To this day, it gives me joy to think of how I saw them zealously pursue peace and end in peace. A few weeks after the case ended, they surprised me by honoring me before my church's elder board. I am black; they are white. I mention race as it became particularly relevant in May 2020.

On May 25, 2020, a white policeman killed a black man, George Floyd, which heightened racial unrest with much of the country divided on racial lines. I believe every Christian has a duty to help regarding racial conciliation and other conciliation. During that time, people were lumping races of people in one basket. No one should lump everyone in any race in a general basket of one-size-fits-all. I thought about my white brothers during the George Floyd protest and how God allowed us to partner together in disregard of race. I wrote them about the disheartening racial unrest and expressed appreciation for how we worked together in disregard of race. They responded in a similar vein.

CONFRONTATION IS SOMETIMES NECESSARY IN RESOLUTION LAND

Sometimes confrontation is necessary and the right thing to do. In another situation of working with a white person, it did not start well but ended well. The person is a Christian but discriminated against me. He did many things that people refer to as culturally insensitive, some glaringly egregious. I have worked in conflict resolution for over 30 years and felt that I needed to resolve the matter appropriately, so I requested a meeting. I kept in mind that he is a fellow-image bearer of Christ but had engaged in unacceptable behavior. I told him I would like to meet with him regarding what I experienced while working with him.

Confrontation requires us to restore a person gently, "Brothers and sisters, if someone is caught in a sin, you who live by the Spirit should restore that person gently. But watch yourselves, or you also may be tempted" (Galatians 6:1). Gentleness does not mean being slack, possibly leading to the person's failure to recognize the need for repentance. In addition, the person confronting should examine themselves and confront with the right attitude and heart without self-righteousness. Speak the truth, but do it in love (see Ephesians 4:15).

We teach when we meet regarding a conflict—the first thing to do is validate the person. I gave him true statements of validation; you are my brother in Christ. You have gifts that God uses, which I believe could be used to a greater degree if you correct certain behaviors. I told him my goal was to help, not to harm. I shared indisputable facts and gave it to him in writing so there would be no misunderstanding. I told him I ran the facts through the discrimination elements grid and said his behavior met the legal elements of discrimination.

He did not deny any of the things that happened. He asked me what he could do to make it right. I felt that was a loaded question, not because he intended it to be but because the devil always wants to derail peacemaking efforts. Caveat: Never play God in people's lives. I proceeded cautiously. I told him I recommended that he seek God, pray, and ask God whether his behavior was unconscious bias or conscious disregard, and the Holy Spirit would direct him.

He shared part of his background and told me he grew up in the south and said it would be impossible not to have bias. In a conversational tone, I shared what my dad taught me in the language my dad used "one damned man is not any better than another damned man." I told him God does not respect him any more than he respects me. Diverse groups can work together in unity despite diversity to tear down strongholds and myths and bring greater growth and peace. I had felt compelled by God to meet with him. I am sure that I did not say it all perfectly, but I said it to the best of my ability with a clean heart toward him. We can do our best and trust God with the consequences. When I confronted him, he could have rebuffed me, but he did not. Regardless of a person's response, we have a responsibility to pursue peace.

A BULLY EXPERIENCE

Some people reside in Hostile Land instead of Resolution Land. Some of these are bullies who try to control others. Psychiatrist William Glasser described controlling behavior as "Seven Deadly Habits of External Control Psychology:"

1. Criticizing

2. Blaming

3. Complaining

4. Nagging

5. Threatening

6. Punishing

7. Bribing

You've seen and probably experienced these negative patterns in people and how it fosters conflict. Glasser believed many of these negative behaviors are because a person has social issues and unhappiness in relationships. Healthy, strong relationships help unhappiness and mental health.

Key terms for Glasser's approach and work are "personal choice," "personal responsibility," and "transformation." He took an educational counseling approach to help people with personal choices and help them take personal responsibility for their behavior and personal responsibility for changing it.

Some try to control relationships through the seven hostile behaviors described above. I encountered a bully in a ministry situation who engaged in most if not all seven of the behaviors. He tried to force me to do something ministry-related that was wrong. He verbally browbeat me trying to force me to bend the rules for him or at least tell him how the rules could be bent. He pushed me repeatedly through phone conversations and some e-mails. I prayed and used every peacemaking rule I know. Perhaps he misunderstood my attempt at loving-kindness for weakness. Whatever the case, he was unrelenting and became abusive. I finally said I felt like he was bullying me, and I wasn't having it. He then went to the threatening stage by telling me he would report me to the pastor. I told him this is the last conversation I would have with him without a witness. I did not know him and had never heard of him before that situation. I later learned that he had a bully reputation, and when he wanted his way, nothing would suffice other than his way. Had it not been a church matter, I would not have added: "without a witness."

Being Christian requires us to love and seek peace. It does not require that we allow people to abuse us. Sometimes, a sharp rebuke can be helpful. The apostle Paul instructed the church to sharply rebuke the Cretans for evil behavior (see Titus 1:12-13). Sometimes confrontation is necessary. However, when you have done all you can do for peace, and it does not work, turn the page. Walk away. Leave the person to God and trust God for the consequences of your obedience to Him.

CHAPTER 18

ACTION MUST ACCOMPANY RESOLUTION LAND MINDSET

*"Do not merely listen to the word,
and so deceive yourselves. Do what it says."*

JAMES 1:22

Before the beginning of time, God chose us to be holy, created us to be holy, and tells us to live holy because He is holy. A call to holiness is a call to live righteously.

- "For he chose us in him before the creation of the world to be holy and blameless in his sight. In love" (Ephesians 1:4).

- "But just as he who called you is holy, so be holy in all you do; for it is written: "Be holy, because I am holy" (1 Peter 15:16).

- "Make every effort to live in peace with everyone and to be holy; without holiness no one will see the Lord" (Hebrews 12:14).

- "He has saved us and called us to a holy life-not because of anything we have done but because of his own purpose and grace. This grace was given us in Christ Jesus before the beginning of time" (2 Timothy 1:9).

Unrighteous living and conflict are not the way to live. "A hot-tempered person stirs up conflict, but the one who is patient calms a quarrel" (Proverbs 15:18). For peace, turn away from hot-tempered anger and answer softly (see Proverbs 15:1).

AUTHENTIC CHRISTIAN OR NOT?

During childhood, I loved to watch an old TV game show called "To Tell the Truth." The program consisted of four celebrities on one side and three contestants on the other side. The program's host would read information about the central character, who was one of the three contestants. The other two contestants were imposters claiming to be the central character. To provide a name, let's call the central character Johnny Appleseed. At the beginning of the program, one after another, each contestant would say, my name is Johnny Appleseed. I enjoyed hearing the contestants say the name with different inflections:

> Contestant #1 – My name is Johnny Appleseed
>
> Contestant #2 – My name **is** Johnny Appleseed
>
> Contestant #3 – My name is **Johnny Appleseed**

The host would read biographical information about Johnny Appleseed. Then each celebrity would ask each contestant questions related to the biography to gain enough information to identify the real Johnny Appleseed.

At the end of all the questions, each celebrity would vote on who they believed to be the real Johnny Appleseed, Contestant #1, #2, or #3. Each week I would cast my vote at home as no doubt other viewers cast their votes. After each celebrity shared how they voted, the host would then give the command that I had eagerly waited for, "Will the real Johnny Appleseed, please stand up." Then we would watch as the three contestants would go through playful antics of standing up and sitting down. In the end, only the real Johnny Appleseed would remain standing, and the imposters were exposed.

Do people have to guess whether you are a real Christian? Does your conduct reflect authentic Christianity or an imposter masquerading as a Christian? Real Christians stand up by endeavoring to do right daily. Real Christians stand up by applying biblical principles. We operate in self-deception when we name the name of Christ and do not do what He says (see James 1:22).

OBEY GOD

Real life is not a game show, but where we have life issues. With those issues, we can obey God by pursuing peace and the building up of one another. In a secular court, the judge can order mediation for the disputants to resolve the conflict. The disputants obey the judge by going to mediation because of fear of sanctions. Where is the fear of God, our Supreme Judge? He tells us to pursue peace. However, we dig in our heels from polarized positions of sin and judgment of others without an attempt at reconciliation. God has consequences for disobeying Him far beyond what any other judge can order.

PURSUE PEACE

No arena of society exists free of conflict. Though conflict is unavoidable, the way we handle it is up to us. We need not foster it. Negativity surrounds us; Facebook trolls, Twitter claps back; online bullies, and other adversity. The culture accepts terrible behavior as the norm and seems to enjoy it. As people continue to become desensitized to evil, it continues to escalate. We hear by far more negative news stories than positive ones.

Many express negative opinions and polarize based on those opinions. Petty competition from who wore it best on the red carpet to winning political arguments through vitriol is prevalent. That is not the way we are supposed to live. Where are those who pursue peace per Scripture? Rather than living by the Bible, some seem to live by the book of social media or the book of favorite news station.

Years ago, I walked out the front door of my house and saw a little boy, about six years old, running down the middle of the street toward my house. There was no neighborhood traffic on that quiet afternoon. His facial expression was severe, and his little legs moved robustly. I thought he needed help and was about to intervene until I looked toward where he was running. Then, I understood. He was in hot pursuit of an ice cream truck that was leaving our street!

Pursue means to chase after or run after. Romans 14:9 tells us to pursue peace. Until we want peace and chase after it as heartily as that little boy chased after ice cream, we are not serious enough about pursuing peace. That child was so focused on his goal that he was not distracted and never lost sight of the truck. We too, can pursue peace. We can do it by embracing diversity assignments for the pursuit of holiness and peace. "Let us therefore make every effort to do what leads to peace and to mutual edification" (Romans 14:19).

PLANNED BIBLICAL RESPONSE: CONFIGURATION

I used to work at a bank where I supervised tellers. We had a specific action plan for tellers to follow in the event of a robbery. The plan included ensuring the safety of employees and other rules related to the inconspicuous alarm and marked money. Although we did not know whether we would ever have a robbery, we planned for the event of a robbery. We need to do no less for something we know will come. Having a biblical response plan is essential for inevitable conflicts.

I learned about a planned biblical response from Dallas Seminary Chaplain Bill Bryan. His response plan related to "worry," but you can take the process and apply it to any problem. The process identifies the problem (diagnosis) and then identifies scriptures to resolve the problem (antidote). For purposes of how it works, let's look at a diagnosis and antidote applied to unforgiveness. Many people have unforgiving hearts. The following scriptures on forgiveness will be used in the upcoming example of a Planned Biblical Response.

- "Get rid of all bitterness, rage and anger, brawling and slander, along with every form of malice. Be kind and compassionate to one another, forgiving each other, just as in Christ God forgave you" (Eph 4:31-32).

- "But if you do not forgive others their sins, your Father will not forgive your sins" (Matthew 6:15).

- "Be completely humble and gentle; be patient, bearing with one another in love" (Ephesians 4:2).

- "If we confess our sins, he is faithful and just and will forgive us our sins and purify us from all unrighteousness" (1 John 1:9).

PLANNED BIBLICAL RESPONSE (PBR)

Ephesians 4:31-32, Matthew 6:15, Ephesians 4:2, 1 John 1:9 (Forgive)

Problem of Unforgiveness (Diagnosis)

- We are commanded to forgive (Matthew 6:15, Ephesians 4:32)

- Unforgiveness is disobedience to God

- Unforgiveness is a sin

- Unforgiveness brings a penalty (Matthew 6:15)

Prescription for Unforgiveness (Antidote)

- Obey God; forgive (Ephesians 4:32, Matthew 6:15, Ephesians 4:2)

- Repent (1 John 1:9).

- Turn away from unforgiveness characteristics

  o Bitterness (Ephesians 4:31)

  o Rage (Ephesians 4:31)

  o Anger (Ephesians 4:31)

  o Brawling (Ephesians 4:31)

- o Slander (Ephesians 4:31)

- o Every form of malice (Ephesians 4:31)

- Embrace forgiveness traits

  - o Kindness (Ephesians 4:32)

  - o Compassion (Ephesians 4:31)

  - o Forgiving (like Christ forgave us) (Ephesians 4:31)

  - o Humility (Ephesians 4:2)

  - o Gentleness (Ephesians 4:2)

  - o Patience (Ephesians 4:2)

  - o Bearing with one another (Ephesians 4:2)

  - o Love (Ephesians 4:2)

To set the plan accurately, you only have one choice, "Do the right thing," which automatically takes place when you apply Scripture, the antidote for the diagnosis. God made us free-will beings who can decide to do good or evil. Since we have a choice, we can choose to take only the option of doing good. It is somewhat analogous to computer software. My editing software can check for misspelled words, but it cannot do an online search. It can only do what the software developer configured it to do. In our free will ability, we can decide to exclude evil behavior from our conduct. You might say we are not robots. Of course not. We have a choice, which means we are not forced to either position. Computers have glitches that can be fixed, and people have glitches that can be fixed. Repent; turn away from sin; get back on track.

A friend and I discussed how some people swear at or make negative comments when other drivers cut them off in traffic. I suggested that people say, "God bless you," instead. They said the mind is not that quick to come up with "God bless you." You prove the mind is that quick when you immediately swear at people who cut you off in traffic. If the mind is quick for evil, it can be quick for good. We merely need to renew our minds with the correct configuration. Our configuration is misaligned because of our sinful nature and learned behavior. When we renew our minds in accordance with Scripture, we reconfigure. "Do not conform to the pattern of this world, but be transformed by the renewing of your mind. Then you will be able to test and approve what God's will is—his good, pleasing and perfect will" (Romans 12:2). Spiritual growth is also part of reconfiguring. Some married couples establish upfront that divorce is off the table. They configure to stay married. You also can decide that ungodly behavior is off the table during the multitude of diversity assignments. Bring glory to God during conflict encounters by applying Scripture to bring peace and unity.

FOLLOW THE MATTHEW BRICK ROAD

The Bible gives specific steps for addressing sinful conflict. The steps show the path to follow. In the Wizard of Oz, Dorothy did not know the way to Emerald City but received directions to "follow the yellow brick road." For our conflict resolution journey, we go to our biblical GPS to navigate the way to our peaceful destination. Our navigation system takes us to what I refer to as the Matthew Brick Road, Matthew 18:15-17. It is part of our planned response.

Matthew 18:15

The first leg of the journey is Matthew 18:15. It tells us what to do and who to talk to regarding the matter. "If your brother or sister sins, go and point out their fault, just between the two of you. If they listen to you, you have won them over" (Matthew 18:15 NLT). Let's unpack verse 15.

- The words "brother or sister" denote that we are talking about fellow believers.

- What does the verse tell us about your brother or sister? They sinned; violated God's Word.

- Who did they sin against? You.

- The verse directs you to act, i.e., "Go," which depicts a personal responsibility to act.

- Where are you going? To the person who sinned against you.

- Why are you going? To show the person their fault (how they sinned against you).

- Who goes with you? No one. Keep it private, just between the two of you.

- What is your goal for going? To get them to repent; win them over; resolve the matter.

In Matthew 18:15, the only two people who are supposed to be involved are you and the person who sinned again you. That resolves the matter at the lowest possible level without telling others. When each side tells others, they generally tell their friends in a light most favorable to them. The friends, who should not be involved, then polarize against the other person based on their friend's version. Interestingly, the other side does the same. Each side polarizes against the other, having heard a different version about the same dispute. That is why it is important not to involve others. Keep peace; don't spread the matter.

When you "go," to the other person, your tone, demeanor, and attitude are important for a peaceful resolution. Lovingly speak the truth to the person. "Instead, speaking the truth in love, we will grow to become in every respect the mature body of him who is the head, that is, Christ" (Ephesians 4:15). You have a personal responsibility to privately carry out the mandate to act when a brother or sister sins against you. If the person listens, it ends there. The word "listens" implies they give a proper response. If they listen to you, you have won them over. That is the goal, repentance from sin and to gain unity.

Matthew 18:16

If the person does not listen, move to the second leg of the Matthew Brick Road journey, Matthew 18:16. "But if they will not listen, take one or two others along, so that every matter may be established by the testimony of two or three witnesses" (Matthew 18:16).

- Verse 16 also directs you to act, i.e., take one or two with you, which shows a continuing personal responsibility to act by taking one or two with you.

- Where are you going? Back to the person that you went to alone at Matthew 18:15

- Why are you going? To show the person their fault (how they sinned against you); same as Matthew 18:15.

- Who goes with you? One or two people.

- What is the role of the one or two others? To be witnesses to the matter to establish the matter.

- What is the goal? Get them to repent.

Matthew 18:16 is a continuing personal responsibility to pursue resolution, though you request other believers to assist as objective witnesses. "But if they will not listen, take one or two others along, so that every matter may be established by the testimony of two or three witnesses" (Matthew 18:16). Every matter must be established by the testimony of two or three witnesses (see Deuteronomy 9:15, Matthew 18:16, 2 Corinthians 13:1). The weight of the evidence scales is heavier with two or three witnesses than with one person, as prescribed in the immediately preceding scriptural references.

It is essential that you take trustworthy people with you—those who have a good reputation and are known for being peacemakers. Otherwise, you potentially exacerbate the matter and end up with greater conflict. Also, the person you confront may not trust the process if you take one of your friends with you. If the person listens and repents, then the journey ends, and no further action is needed. Note that involving one or two additional people still keeps the number of people involved at a minimum.

Both Matthew 18:15 and Matthew 18:16 encourage repentance. At each stage, remember to treat the person with respect and dignity. God requires us to bear with one another and forgive one another's offenses (see Colossians 3:13). Do not condemn, but lovingly speak the truth to the person. Follow the golden rule and speak to them in the way you would desire to be spoken to if the roles were reversed. "In everything, do to others what you would have them do to you, for this sums up the Law and the Prophets" (Matthew 7:12).

Both verses presuppose that you were the person wronged. That may not be the case. Perhaps you have a log in your eye and did not see clearly. Be open to correction. Each believer has a personal responsibility to help fellow believers turn from sin after he has repented of his own sin. Thus, the prerequisite to go to another to point out their sin is that you have first corrected your own sins. "You hypocrite, first take the plank out of your own eye, and then you will see clearly to remove the speck from your brother's eye" (Matthew 7:5).

Matthew 18:17 - Tell It to the Church

If the person does not listen at Matthew 18:16, move to the last leg of the journey, Matthew 18:17. "If they still refuse to listen, tell it to the church; and if they refuse to listen even to the church, treat them as you would a pagan or a tax collector" (Matthew 18:17).

God gave the church legal authority to operate on His behalf. According to 1 Corinthians 6, the church operates as a court in such matters. At Matthew 18:17, church leadership encourages repentance and may take disciplinary if the person continues to refuse to repent. Without church discipline, sin in the church will continue to compromise the unity and testimony of God's people.[30] If the person repents before disciplinary action takes place, the process ends, except the church may provide supportive measures, like counseling, support group, accountability care, or other support. The goal is correction for spiritual well-being, not punishment.

WATCH YOUR THOUGHTS AND WORDS

Two critical areas that impact resolution are our words and thoughts. God gave us the written Word (Scripture), the living Word (Jesus), and the spoken Word.

Words

Never underestimate the power of what we say. "The tongue has the power of life and death, and those who love it will eat its fruit" (Proverbs 18:21). We can speak death or life. Even the secular culture recognizes the benefit of positive affirmations. Though positive affirmations can be helpful, they don't have the power of God's Word that gives life. You can remind yourself of Scripture and speak it. We are more than a conqueror through Christ.

> No, in all these things we are more than conquerors through him who loved us. For I am convinced that neither death nor life, neither angels nor demons, neither the present nor the future, nor any powers, neither height nor depth, nor anything else in all creation, will be able to separate us from the love of God that is in Christ Jesus our Lord (Romans 8:37-39).

You can wound the spirit of a child with words or lift up the child's countenance with the right words. Likewise, you can do the same for others and yourself. Encourage yourself. "Instead, be filled with the Spirit, speaking to one another with psalms, hymns, and songs from the Spirit. Sing and make music from your heart to the Lord, always giving thanks to God the Father for everything, in the name of our Lord Jesus Christ" (Ephesians 5:19-20).

There is power in speaking God's Word (see Hebrews 4:12). The weather in Texas can swelter in July and August. Over 30 years ago, in the scorching Texas heat, my home air-conditioning system went out and it was beyond repair. I did not have the funds to buy a new one. My pastor had preached a sermon that we own nothing. It all belongs to God. I became acutely aware that the air conditioner in the house belonged to God. You might think I was delirious from the summer heat, but I was dead serious that miserably hot day when I cried out, "God, Your air conditioner is broken; what are You going to do about it?" I meant every word of it, just the way I said it. I was in desperate need with no other avenue. Shortly afterward, I received a large check in the mail that I had forgotten was owed to me. It was enough to get a new air-conditioning and heating system with money left over.

I had reminded God that He owns that air conditioner, and I was just a steward over His property. I know the sun shines on everyone, and it rains on everyone (see Matthew 5:45). However, that does not stop us from trusting God and living a life of faith. I knew God owned the air conditioner, and I faithfully believed He would do something about His air conditioner. He did.

We cannot control God, but much happens according to the faith we exercise. Reflect on Shadrach, Meshach, and Abednego (see Daniel 3:16-28). These three men were thrown in a furnace of fire because they refused to bow in worship to the golden image contrary to the king's decree. The king brought them forth to explain why they would not bow to the golden image as he required. Their answer seems contradictory.

> They replied to him, "King Nebuchadnezzar, we do not need to defend ourselves before you in this matter. If we are thrown into the blazing furnace, the God we serve is able to deliver us from it, and he will deliver us from Your Majesty's hand. But even if he does not, we want you to know, Your Majesty, that we will not serve your gods or worship the image of gold you have set up (Daniel 3:16-18).

To say, He "will" deliver us seems inconsistent with also saying, "but if not." It is not inconsistent. Their statement showed their faith (He will) and also recognized God's sovereignty (but if not). Though we can have faith, the answer is always God's. We can speak the Word, trust God, but never forget only He is sovereign. God's sovereignty refers to His absolute rule and control of the universe and all in it. He alone is God. He is the King, we are His subjects. We can rest in the fact that whatever decision God makes, He works it out for our good (See Roman 8:28).

Thoughts

The mind is said to be the devil's playing field. Our thoughts have a significant impact on our lives. Scripture tells us, we are what we think. "For as he thinks in his heart, so is he" (Proverbs 23:7 NKJV). Our behavior, good and bad, starts with thoughts. If you entertain evil thoughts, you will likely end in bad behavior. Don't let the devil take up residency in your mind with his evilness and trickery.

We frequently talk to ourselves, through our thoughts. Some of that self-talk is destructive, discouraging, defeatist talk. For example, telling yourself what you can't accomplish instead of faithfully believing and pursing your dreams. Cease "I can't do it" thoughts that are contrary to what God says about us, "I can do all this through him who gives me strength" (Philippians 4:13). In *Transformed Through His Thoughts*, Dr. Guy Earle gives a practical guide to help reprogram your mind with God's thoughts from Scripture leaving destructive thoughts for productive thoughts.

Romans 12 instructs us to renew our minds. "Do not conform to the pattern of this world, but be transformed by the renewing of your mind. Then you will be able to test and approve what God's will is—his good, pleasing and perfect will" (Romans 12:2). We renew our minds with Scripture. We can control our thoughts and take them captive. "We demolish arguments and every pretension that sets itself up against the knowledge of God, and we take captive every thought to make it obedient to Christ" (2 Corinthians 10:5). Defeat the greatest impediment to your success, your own thoughts. Do so by renewing your mind with God's Word to change from destructive self-talk to productive self-talk.

Peace and unity are so important that God does not want us to worship at the altar when we have uncorrected sinned against someone (see Matthew 5:24). Bear with one another and allow for differing perspectives. Follow the Matthew Brick Road, your Planned Biblical Response, and watch your words and thoughts.

As you carry out your Planned Biblical Response, separate the person from their behavior, discussed in the Relationships and Social Interactions chapter, summarized here:

The Encounter: An Assignment from God

You: Embrace the ministry of reconciliation assignment to handle it in a God-honoring way.

The Person: Separate the fellow-image bearer from their behavior. Bear with them and treat them with respect and dignity.

The Issue/Conduct: Determine whether the issue is a differing opinion or a sin. Allow for different perspectives. Do not violate God's standards. Embrace/accept the person; reject sinful conduct.

Love: Be mindful to keep love in the forefront as directed by the two greatest commandments.

Below are six additional points to keep in mind as you pursue reconciled relationships.

Point 1: "Have proper regard for all people." Recognize that humans are made in God's image and thus are valuable beings.

Point 2: "Treat people with respect and dignity." We treat valuables with care, like our fine jewelry and other valuables. Every person is more valuable than our most precious material good.

Point 3: "Let who you are dictate your actions." If you profess Christ, your identity is in Him and you are His ambassador. Let who you are guide your behavior.

Point 4: "Let your actions show love." The two greatest commandments center around fervent love for God and love of each other (See Matthew 22:36-40). Love is an action.

Point 5: "Watch your words." Sometimes physical wounds can heal faster than harsh words that sting and bring deep hurt. Speak to build up and encourage each other, not tear down. A soft response turns anger away (see Proverbs 15:1).

Point 6: "Allow for the differences of others." Differences of opinions or perspectives should not cause war. You and others are entitled to differ. You are each original and unique, worth more than a copy.

Point 7: Commit to serve as a minister of reconciliation to resolve personal conflict and help others resolve conflict (see 2 Corinthians 5:17-18, Romans 12:18).

We have come to the end of our learning journey through *Diversity of a Different Kind*, a different perspective and approach to resolve conflict. We interact with over a dozen differences common to man; spiritual gifts, personality, learning styles, race, generational, gender, religion, politics, responses to conflict, capacity to manage conflict, socioeconomics, education, family, and other life experiences.

God has set His love on us, made us in His image and breathed life into us. He plans to prosper us not harm us (see Jeremiah 29:11). His goal for us is to make us holy and He lovingly superintends our growth. He set up a diverse system for us to grow, where we can use naturally arising opportunities to practice biblical principles to produce Christlike character growth.

We can embrace the naturally arising assignments for our benefit of growth and unity and impede the devil's goal for disunity and disruption of our lives, families, ministries, and society. As we said throughout the book, "He set us up to grow us up." God loves diversity and we can change our mindsets to embrace the beauty of it all; the encounters, the broadening of our horizons, and insights into life beyond narrow avenues.

When you look at your child, you smile lovingly. When God looks at His obedient children, He does the same for every one of His diverse image-bearers, from every nation, tribe, and tongue with various changeable and unchangeable differences. One day we will all stand together in one place: "After this I looked, and there before me was a great multitude that no one could count, from every nation, tribe, people and language, standing before the throne and before the Lamb. They were wearing white robes and were holding palm branches in their hands" (Revelation 7:9).

In a bygone era, movie directors would call for action on the movie set before they rolled the camera. The acting would then start and ended when the director pronounced "cut." At the end of our life journey, God will pronounce "cut" and our time on this side of eternity is done. I end this book by reminding you of the last two lines of the poem "Differences." The chief aim of life should be to bring Him glory. When it's all said and done, what will be your story?

GLOSSARY

Diversity of a Different Kind coins several phrases related to its unique viewpoint to resolve diversity conflict.

Diversity perspective is the view that God designed diversity to grow us into Christlikeness.

Diversity approach is to have a heart to embrace God's divine design of diversity for its benefit.

Diversity theory is the belief that God created human diversity to give us naturally arising opportunities to practice biblical principles to produce Christlike character growth.

Diversity encounter is a divine assignment from God, which gives us opportunities to practice biblical principles for growth.

Diversity rub is sinful intolerance of others and their differences.

Diversity embrace is defined as godly tolerance of others and their differences.

Destructive conflict management aligns with diversity rub, which is sinful intolerance of others and their differences.

Constructive conflict management aligns with diversity embrace, which is godly tolerance of others and their differences.

Living in "Resolution Land" is a non-physical location where you have an ongoing mindset to pursue peace and harmony with others. It is a mindset and attitude that brings peacemaking action.

CONFLICT MANAGEMENT CAPACITY CATEGORIES AND DESCRIPTIONS (ROMANS 15:1-4)

Desires peace refers to having a heart for peace.

Conflict management capable—desires peace and is able to work positively toward conflict resolution. This person is spiritually mature and generally acts righteously. However, no person is perfect and can miss the mark periodically.

Conflict management capable with support—desires peace but at times may need conflict coaching support to resolve conflict. Feelings can be raw, and conflicted parties may need a neutral third party to assist them. As ministers of reconciliation, more mature believers can serve as mediators to help resolve the matter. And recall that Christ is the mediator between God and all, "For there is one God and one mediator between God and mankind, the man Christ Jesus" (1 Timothy 2:5).

Conflict management capable with limitations—desires peace but struggles during interactions with others. This person can often be helped in several ways, including mediation, training, heightened awareness of the need to obey God, and spiritual growth.

Conflict management incapable at this time—does not desire peace. Appears to thrive in chaos, unwilling or unable to resolve conflict. The person may be so wounded or so spiritually immature or unspiritual they need time. Pray for them and model the way.

NOTES

1. Inner Circle Band, "Bad Boys" (1987)

2. McGee, Robert, *The Search for Significance*, 2003.

3. Lesslie Newbigin (1909-1998), *Truth and Authority in Modernity*. (Gracewing, 1996) 38-39.

4. Christian Educator's Journal, April 2008).

5. Eye of the Beholder (The Twilight Zone, 1959) - Wikipedia

6. Eye of the Beholder (The Twilight Zone, 1959) - Wikipedia

7. There is beauty in a gap-tooth! | LivinginDiaspora (wordpress.com)

8. Taylor, S. (2018). The Psychology of Racism | Psychology Today

9. Azarian, B. (2018). Understanding the Racist Brain | Psychology Today

10. Evans, Tony. Oneness Embraced (p. 18). Moody Publishers. Kindle Edition.

11. Manser, M. H. (2009). *Dictionary of Bible Themes: The Accessible and Comprehensive Tool for Topical Studies*. London: Martin Manser.

12. Thomas, Gary. 2000. *Sacred Marriage*. Zondervan.

13. William Killgore, Mika Oki, and Deborah Yurgelum-Todd, "Sex-Specific Developmental Changes in Amygdala

14. Janet Lever, "Sex Differences in the Games Children Play," Social Problems, 23:478-87, 1976.

15. Lizette Peterson, Tammy Brazeal, Krista Oliver and Cathy Bull, "Gender and Developmental Patterns of Affect. Belief and Behavior in Simulated Injury Events." Journal of Applied Developmental Psychology, 18:531-46, 1997.

16. Annis, Michael Gurian with Barbara. 2008. *Leadership and the Sexes*. San Francisco: Jossey-Bass.

17. Edwards, Sue and Kelley Matthews. *Leading Women Who Wound*. Chicago: Moody Press, 2009

18. Edwards, Sue and Kelley Matthews. *Leading Women Who Wound*. Chicago: Moody Press, 2009

19. Taibbi, Robert (2019). 4 Key Ways Your Childhood Shapes You | Psychology Today

20. Dr. Tony Evans Speaks From His Heart About Social Injustice - YouTube

21. Carbonell, Mels. 2003. *Discovering Your Giftedness*. Blue Ridge: Uniquely You Resources.

22. Eph 5:15-21; Romans 6:12-13; Acts 9:17-20; Chafer pp 40-44; Walvoord, John F.; Zuck, Roy B.; Dallas Theological Seminary: *The Bible Knowledge Commentary: An Exposition of the Scriptures*. Wheaton, IL: Victor Books.

23. Ephesians 4:30; Walvoord, John F.; Zuck, Roy B.; Dallas Theological Seminary: *The Bible Knowledge Commentary: An Exposition of the Scriptures*. Wheaton, IL: Victor Books. *College Press NIV Commentary: Galatians and Ephesians*.

24. I Thess. 5:12-22; Walvoord, John F.; Zuck, Roy B.; Dallas Theological Seminary: *The Bible Knowledge Commentary: An Exposition of the Scriptures*. Wheaton, IL: Victor Books, 1983-c1985, S. 2:640. John F.; Zuck, Roy B.; *The Bible Knowledge Commentary: An Exposition of the Scriptures*. Wheaton, IL: Victor Books.

25. Philippians 2:3; Hebrews 13:21; Lewis Sperry. *He That is Spiritual.* Grand Rapids, Michigan: Zondervan, 1967.

26. Galatians 5:16; Chafer, Lewis Sperry. *He That Is Spiritual.* Grand Rapids, Michigan: Zondervan, 1967.

27. Galatians 5:16; Eph 2:3; II Peter 2:18; I John 2:16; Romans 13:14; Chafer, Lewis Sperry. *He That Is Spiritual.* Grand Rapids, Michigan: Zondervan, 1967.

28. (Swindoll 2003)

29. Sims, Jean Stubblefield. *His Will-Not Mine.* 2003.

30. Blomberg, C. (1992). *Matthew* (Vol. 22, p. 280). Nashville: Broadman & Holman Publishers.

ABOUT THE AUTHOR

Oletha Barnett is a theologian, lawyer, and conflict resolution specialist who has directed the conflict resolution ministry at Oak Cliff Bible Fellowship in Dallas, TX for decades. She was commissioned by the Elder Board for conflict resolution work. She is also an adjunct professor at Southern Bible Institute & College, and founder of Conciliation Services LLC, which provides services to churches, other organizations, and individuals.

She serves on the Board of Peacemaker Ministries, is a Certified Christian Conciliator™, Certified Management Specialist, Certified in Christian Prevention Relationship Enhancement, and Certified Human Behavior Consultant. She holds a BS in Mathematics, Juris Doctor, and Master of Arts in Christian Education from Dallas Theological Seminary.

Made in United States
North Haven, CT
14 September 2023

41538600R00102